Miss Linley of Bath

*A Play in Three Acts
by Mary Sheridan* . .

COPYRIGHT, 1936, BY SAMUEL FRENCH, LTD.
All rights reserved

SAMUEL FRENCH, LTD.
26 SOUTHAMPTON STREET, STRAND, LONDON, W.C.2
59 CROSS STREET, MANCHESTER
SAMUEL FRENCH, INC.
25 WEST 45TH STREET, NEW YORK, U.S.A.
811 WEST 7TH STREET, LOS ANGELES, CAL.
SAMUEL FRENCH (CANADA), LTD.
480 UNIVERSITY AVENUE, TORONTO

Copyright © 1936 by Samuel French Ltd
All Rights Reserved

MISS LINLEY OF BATH is fully protected under the copyright laws of the British Commonwealth, including Canada, the United States of America, and all other countries of the Copyright Union. All rights, including professional and amateur stage productions, recitation, lecturing, public reading, motion picture, radio broadcasting, television and the rights of translation into foreign languages are strictly reserved.

ISBN 978-0-573-12215-6

www.samuelfrench.co.uk
www.samuelfrench.com

FOR AMATEUR PRODUCTION ENQUIRIES

UNITED KINGDOM AND WORLD
EXCLUDING NORTH AMERICA
plays@SamuelFrench-London.co.uk
020 7255 4302/01

Each title is subject to availability from Samuel French,
depending upon country of performance.

CAUTION: Professional and amateur producers are hereby warned that MISS LINLEY OF BATH is subject to a licensing fee. Publication of this play does not imply availability for performance. Both amateurs and professionals considering a production are strongly advised to apply to the appropriate agent before starting rehearsals, advertising, or booking a theatre. A licensing fee must be paid whether the title is presented for charity or gain and whether or not admission is charged.

The professional rights in this play are controlled by Samuel French Ltd, 52 Fitzroy Street, London, W1T 5JR.

No one shall make any changes in this title for the purpose of production. No part of this book may be reproduced, stored in a retrieval system, or transmitted in any form, by any means, now known or yet to be invented, including mechanical, electronic, photocopying, recording, videotaping, or otherwise, without the prior written permission of the publisher. No one shall upload this title, or part of this title, to any social media websites.

The right of Mary Sheridan to be identified as author of this work has been asserted in accordance with Section 77 of the Copyright, Designs and Patents Act 1988.

MISS LINLEY OF BATH

Produced at the "Playhouse," Liverpool, on October 30th, 1935, with the following cast of characters:

(In the order of their appearance)

THOMAS LINLEY	James Stephenson.
ALICIA SHERIDAN	Louise Frodsham.
POLLY LINLEY	Betty Fleetwood.
ELIZABETH ANN LINLEY	Rachael Kempson.
MARY LINLEY	Pauline Lacey.
THOMAS MATTHEWS	Stephen Jack.
SHELAH O'GRADY	Deirdre Doyle.
THOMAS SHERIDAN	Lloyd Pearson.
RICHARD BRINSLEY SHERIDAN	Michael Redgrave.
CHARLES SHERIDAN	Denis Webb.
EDWARD KNIGHT	John Kidd.
MÈRE MARIE JOSEPH	Eileen Douglas.
MONSIEUR LE CURÉ	Alfred Sangster.
LANDLORD	Cyril Lister.

Settings by CHARLES THOMAS.

The play was produced by WILLIAM ARMSTRONG.

SYNOPSIS OF SCENES

The action takes place during the springtime of 1772.

ACT I

SCENE 1.—A room at Mr. Linley's house at Bath, March 17th.
SCENE 2.—The same, next evening.

ACT II

SCENE 1.—The parlour of a convent in France. Morning, two weeks later.
SCENE 2.—A room at the White Hart Inn, Bath. Night, four days later.

ACT III

SCENE 1.—A room at Mr. Sheridan's lodgings. Next evening.
SCENE 2.—The same. A week later.

MISS LINLEY OF BATH

ACT I

SCENE 1

SCENE.—*A room at* MR. LINLEY'S *house in Bath.*
It is a large room, sparsely furnished. There are two doors, that on the L. *leading to the living-room of the house, that on the* R. *to the entrance hall. The windows are* R.C. *and* L.C. *in the back wall. There is a harpsichord to the* L. *of the room and a settee to the* R. *A cabinet, a small table, and a few chairs and stools complete the furniture.*
(*See Ground Plan of Scene.*)
The living-room, beyond, is full of children (ten of MR. LINLEY'S *twelve children are in the house) and whenever the door to the* L. *opens, one hears small babies crying, larger babies practising on musical instruments, and pet dogs barking.*

As the play opens THOMAS LINLEY *is giving* ALICIA SHERIDAN *a singing lesson, along with his two daughters* ELIZABETH *and* POLLY, *who have been included to act as an encouragement. Before the* CURTAIN *rises we hear the lesson in progress, first* MR. LINLEY'S *harpsichord accompaniment, then* ELIZABETH'S *" lovely pure soprano " (as Fanny Burney called it), then* ALICIA'S *poor, tuneless quaver, and lastly* POLLY'S *sweet, confident piping. They are singing the round—*

"Summer is icumen in,
Loudly sing cuckoo——"

Half-way through, ALICIA *sings a very obvious false note.* MR. LINLEY *raps impatiently on the harpsichord. There is immediate silence.*

LINLEY. No, no, no, Miss Sheridan! That will never do!

The CURTAIN *rises.* LINLEY *is sitting on a stool in front of the harpsichord. He is a tall, handsome man of thirty-eight, dressed with extreme correctitude. The three girls, looking very young and virginal in their fresh muslins, are standing in a line facing him,* ALICIA *between the two* LINLEYS.

ELIZABETH *is seventeen and supremely beautiful. She is of medium height, and slender, and she has dark eyes and hair. Her manner is gentle and unassuming; her expression candid and sweet. Standing with her eyes demurely cast down, she seems as remote and passionless as an angel. When she raises her eyes, we see that she is a warm, eager young woman.*

ALICIA *is seventeen also. She is plain and inclined to plumpness. Between the two exquisite* LINLEYS, *she appears to be made of distressingly ordinary clay. She has two beauties, however, of which she is inordinately proud, her hair and her small well-shaped hands. All the* SHERIDANS *have the same sort of hair, thick, dark brown and curly.* ALICIA'S *is taken back from her brow and falls over her shoulders in long, natural ringlets. She has no ear for music, and this lesson is anything but pleasant to her. She has a strained, anxious, suffering expression, and her mind is obviously distracted.*

POLLY *is twelve. She is a fair, fragile child with blue eyes. Her hair is tied up with a blue ribbon, and she wears a blue sash. In most ways she is quite as young and innocent as she looks.*

LINLEY (*striking a note and singing*). Miss Sheridan, "Sing cuckoo." You hear? "Sing cuckoo." You have only to listen carefully to Elizabeth, and then repeat the phrase. Try once more.

(ELIZABETH *heaves a little sigh.*)

ALICIA (*tearfully*). I am trying.
LINLEY (*briefly*). Then try a little harder. . . . Now, Elizabeth. (*He begins to play again.*)

ELIZABETH (*singing listlessly*).
"Summer is icumen in,
Loudly sing cuckoo——"
LINLEY. Now, Miss Sheridan——!
ALICIA (*singing*). "Summer is icumen in,
Loudly sing cuckoo."
POLLY (*joining in*). "Summer is icumen in,
Loudly sing cuckoo."
(ALICIA *becomes confused again*.)

LINLEY. No, no, no, Miss Sheridan! Where are your wits this morning? If you don't pay attention to what I tell you, how can you ever hope to learn to sing?

ALICIA (*wailing*). I am paying attention.

LINLEY (*sternly*). I beg your pardon, Madam!

(ELIZABETH *and* POLLY *fidget and sigh*.)

Your attention is quite evidently distracted. It is not even as if you had any gift for singing. Your musical sense is of the most primitive. My daughters, whose talents are of the rarest, are paying you an excessive compliment in singing with you at all. Try not to waste their time as well as mine and your own.

ALICIA (*resentfully*). Your daughters, sir, are public performers, which I have no wish to be.

POLLY (*hurt*). Lissy!

ALICIA. Oh, dear, I didn't mean to say that.

ELIZABETH (*proudly*). Neither have I any wish to be a public performer. I hate it. You know that.

LINLEY. Silence! You have no right to express yourself in such terms in my presence, Elizabeth. You should only be grateful that your father has been able to foster the talent that God gave you.

ELIZABETH. I'm sorry, Papa.

LINLEY. As for you, Miss Sheridan. You seem to forget that your own father is a public performer—and the status of a singer is vastly superior to that of an actor.

ALICIA (*hotly*). Our family is descended from kings!

LINLEY. True! True! The very last time I saw your father, he was Prince of Denmark.

ALICIA (*crossing below to* R. *and bursting into tears*). Oh, I don't want to learn singing. I want to go home.

ELIZABETH (*crossing above to* R.). Whatever is the matter, Lissy?

(POLLY *moves over to* R.C.)

ALICIA (R., *sobbing*). I have a toothache—an insupportable toothache.

ELIZABETH (L. *of* ALICIA). You poor girl! Has it begun again? Why didn't you tell us?

POLLY (*above the settee*). I'll get you a bag of hot salt?

LINLEY (*impatiently—rising*). A toothache indeed! And why, may I ask, should she choose to inflict her ailments upon her music master? Are there not enough dentists in Bath? (*He moves up* C.)

POLLY (R.C.). She is afraid to have it out, Papa. It is a great big one.

LINLEY (L.C.). Stuff and nonsense! It will have to come out sooner or later.

ELIZABETH. Mama has some laudanum in her cupboard upstairs. I will fetch it. (*Trying to seat her on the settee*.) Sit down here, Alicia.

LINLEY. Please conduct your friend to the other apartment, Elizabeth.

(ELIZABETH *and* ALICIA *begin to move* L.)

You know these domestic scenes only distress me.

ELIZABETH. Come in here, Lissy.

(*They go out* L. *into the living-room*.)

LINLEY (*fuming—crossing down* R.). Women have no courage!

POLLY (C., *innocently*). Mama says ladies are much braver than gentlemen.

LINLEY. Indeed!

POLLY (*up* C.). Mama says no gentleman she knows would have had ten children.

LINLEY (*crossing up* R. *of settee to* C.). Polly! That is a most unbecoming observation for a young girl to make.

POLLY. But Mama said——

LINLEY. That is enough.

POLLY (*crestfallen*). Yes, Papa.

(MRS. LINLEY *comes in* L. *She is a stout, talkative lady of forty. She has very definite opinions on every subject. She wears a cap indoors, and is seldom seen without her snuff-box.*)

MRS. LINLEY (L.). Has Polly been saying something to upset you, Thomas?

POLLY (*eager to explain*). I only said——

LINLEY (*moving up* L.). It was nothing, nothing!

(*There is a knock at the front door off* R.)

MRS. LINLEY. Can you see who that is, Polly? (*Moving up* L.C.) I'm not dressed to receive visitors——

POLLY (*peeping out of the window* R.C.). It is a servant knocking, but a gentleman is just getting out of a sedan chair. He is wearing a scarlet coat.

MRS. LINLEY. A scarlet coat?

POLLY. It looks like that Captain Matthews who used to visit us last year.

MRS. LINLEY (*stepping* L.). Captain Matthews!

(LINLEY *picks up his music from the harpsichord.*)

If he has returned to Bath we shall have some proper whist at last! Run and open the door, Polly.

(POLLY *goes out* R.)

Oh, dear! And I in my oldest gown! Where are you going, Mr. Linley!

LINLEY. I have no wish to spend the rest of the morning listening to that fellow talking about himself. I'm going to see how young Tom is progressing with his violin practice. Kindly make my excuses. (*He goes towards the door* L.)

Mrs. Linley (*crossly*). You are behaving exceedingly unsociable, Mr. Linley——

(*He has gone.*)

Dear me! Men!

(Polly *and* Thomas Matthews *come in* R. Matthews *is a dark, handsome, dashing young man of twenty-eight, wearing military uniform. He looks round the room quickly before he greets* Mrs. Linley, *who is beaming with pleasure.* Polly *stands gazing at him in some curiosity.*)

Matthews (*above settee* R.C., *bowing*). Mrs. Linley! Your servant, Ma'am!

Mrs. Linley. Captain Matthews! (*She crosses and gives him her hand to kiss.*) Indeed I am excessively glad to see you. There is not a soul in Bath this winter who can play whist—what *we* call whist, that is. We have awaited your arrival with the greatest eagerness. (*She crosses and sits at* R. *end of the settee.*) We must arrange some rubbers at once . . . (*She sits down and motions him to do the same.*) I trust Mrs. Matthews is well.

Matthews (*with reserve*). Tolerably well, Ma'am. (*He sits at* L. *end of settee.*)

(Polly *stands above the settee.*)

Mrs. Linley. Has she come to Bath with you?

Matthews. No. She prefers to remain in Wales. The climate of Bath does not agree with her.

Mrs. Linley. What a pity, since it suits you so admirably. It *is* good to see you again! You are just in time for Mr. Linley's benefit concert next week. You must take some tickets.

Matthews. Certainly.

Mrs. Linley. Run upstairs and get some, Polly.

(Polly *crosses and goes out* L.)

Matthews. Are all the children performing?

MRS. LINLEY. All except the baby, and the twins who are too young yet. They have been rehearsing this last month. Little Thomas promises to be one of the first violinists of his time.

MATTHEWS. And will Miss Linley be singing?

MRS. LINLEY. Three Miss Linleys will be singing.

MATTHEWS. I meant—Miss Elizabeth.

MRS. LINLEY. Oh, there would not be a concert without Elizabeth. Do you know, Captain Matthews, she is quite the rage this season! (*She laughs at the absurdity of it.*) They call her the maid of Bath. The Maid of Bath—our Betsy!

MATTHEWS (*slowly*). She always promised to be beautiful. (*He goes on, more lightly.*) It seems only a few weeks since she was a child like Polly. So she is grown up now. " The Maid of Bath." Well, well!

MRS. LINLEY. She is seventeen. Of course, I was very young when I married, Captain Matthews.

MATTHEWS (*meaningly*). No one would believe you were Miss Elizabeth's mother!

MRS. LINLEY (*delighted*). Oh, Captain Matthews! I'm afraid you are a sorry tease. (*She laughs.*) But you must really refrain from saying things like that to Elizabeth. She is too young to know different. Though it is true she has had more experience of the world since you knew her last summer. She has sung at court before the King himself. His Majesty congratulated Mr. Linley upon her performance, and gave him a banknote for a hundred pounds.

MATTHEWS. For Miss Elizabeth?

MRS. LINLEY. Well—he meant it for the family, of course. Mr. Linley thinks—we both think—that Elizabeth is far too young yet to have any money of her own.

MATTHEWS. I see.

MRS. LINLEY. Besides, all the children are indentured apprentices to their father until they are twenty-one. Otherwise Mr. Linley could never rely upon his income. If the children had control of half the money they earn, we should both be completely at their mercy. It is a strange world, is it not, Captain Matthews? Elizabeth can earn in one night with her voice more than her father can earn by teaching in a month! We should all be very thankful for her gifts.

MATTHEWS (*dryly*). Yes, indeed.

(POLLY *comes in with a basket. She advances to* MATTHEWS' *side.*)

MRS. LINLEY. Polly sings very charmingly also, Captain Matthews.

MATTHEWS. You must sing for me sometime, moppet. (*He chucks her under the chin.*)

POLLY (C., *distantly*). I do not sing at private parties now, Captain Matthews.

MATTHEWS (*laughing*). Your grown-up airs suit you vastly well, Miss Polly. How old are you?

POLLY (*sulkily*). Twelve.

MATTHEWS. Quite a young woman. Come! (*He pulls her towards him.*) Won't you give a kiss to an old friend?

POLLY (*breaking away angrily*). No!

MRS. LINLEY. Polly! Where are your manners? Kiss the Captain at once.

POLLY (*breaking to* L.). I won't, I won't! I hate old men who try to kiss you.

MRS. LINLEY. Polly!

MATTHEWS (*laughing shortly*). It is the first time I knew twenty-eight was old.

POLLY. You *are* old. Elizabeth says so.

MATTHEWS (*sternly*). Elizabeth!

MRS. LINLEY. You may retire to the other room, Polly. I shall have something to say about this later. Kindly tell your sister that Captain Matthews is here, and that I wish her to join me in the music-room.

POLLY (L.—*rebelliously*). She is with Alicia. (*She puts the basket on the harpsichord.*)

MRS. LINLEY. Hasn't that tiresome girl gone home yet?

POLLY. She's waiting for Shelah to call for her. She has a toothache.

Mrs. Linley. She would have. Do you know the Sheridans, Captain Matthews?

Matthews. Only by repute. They are not exactly my class. The father is a sort of play actor, isn't he?

Mrs. Linley. They are the most fatiguing people—the whole family of them.

Matthews. I did hear that the daughter was no beauty, and the sons were a pair of undisciplined young jackanapes.

Mrs. Linley. Precisely!

Polly (l.c., *hotly*). I like Dick better than any other person in Bath. Dick is a *real* gentleman.

Mrs. Linley (*rising*). Polly! Kindly go at once and inform Elizabeth that I wish her to come here. You need not return.

(Matthews *rises.*)

Polly. Yes, Mama.

(*She goes out* l.)

(*There is a slightly awkward pause.*)

Matthews. Is Mr. Linley not at home?

Mrs. Linley. Er—yes. (*She sits at* r. *end of the settee again.*) He is at home, but he is very busy giving lessons.

(Matthews *sits at* l. *end of settee.*)

I hope you will excuse him.

Matthews (*grandly*). Certainly.

(*There is another pause.*)

Mrs. Linley (*bustling—rising and crossing* r.). I am sure you would like some sherry?

Matthews. Thank you. (*He rises and moves up* l. *of settee.*)

(Elizabeth *comes in* l. *She closes the door and stands against it.* Matthews *jumps to attention. They look at each other for a long moment.*)

MATTHEWS (*bowing*). Miss Linley! Your servant, Ma'am.

(ELIZABETH *drops a slight curtsy.*)

ELIZABETH (L.). Captain Matthews. I—I did not think you were expected until next month.

MATTHEWS (*above* L. *of settee*). I could not bear to be absent from Bath for a moment longer.

MRS. LINLEY (*down* R.). Entertain the Captain, Elizabeth. I must get some wine.

(MATTHEWS *goes above to open the door for her.*)

ELIZABETH. I will go, Mama.

MRS. LINLEY. You would never find it.

(*She goes out* R. *As soon as the door is closed* MATTHEWS *rushes to* ELIZABETH *and takes her hand in his.*)

MATTHEWS. Elizabeth, my love! At last! (*He kisses her hand.*)

ELIZABETH (*withdrawing at once*). Sir!

MATTHEWS (C., *laughing*). Oh, you needn't play the frightened maid with me. I know you too well. Come, we've waited all these months. Kiss me!

ELIZABETH (L.C., *breaking away from him*). Oh, shame, Captain Matthews. (*She moves below him to* R.C.)

MATTHEWS. You were not so shy last summer.

ELIZABETH (R.C.). I was a child then. I did not understand.

MATTHEWS (C.). Child, indeed! You were sixteen and as practised a little coquette as any I ever met.

ELIZABETH. If I gave you that impression, Captain Matthews, I gave it in all innocence. I must ask you not to impose upon my last year's inexperience.

MATTHEWS. Oh! My lady has been to court since last summer; she has sung in a palace, and been ogled by a king!

(ELIZABETH *turns away abruptly and crosses up* R. *of settee.*)

She is setting her cap at a title no doubt. (*Going up* C.

to her.) She wants to forget that once she accepted the adoration of a mere captain of the militia—and returned it.

ELIZABETH. Sir! You go too far!

MATTHEWS (*menacingly*). Can she deny it? Who wrote me a dozen little letters?

ELIZABETH. You are a married man.

MATTHEWS. You knew that last summer.

ELIZABETH. Even your wife could not blame me for the childish affection I gave you. You seemed as old as my father. You—you *know* I meant nothing!

MATTHEWS. It would be a little difficult to persuade other people perhaps.

(ELIZABETH *crosses to above the harpsichord.*)

A word from me whispered to the society of Bath and where would lovely Miss Linley's reputation be? Your father, too—he might not understand that all those stolen meetings in the garden——

ELIZABETH (*distraught*). Captain Matthews, I implore you——

(MRS. LINLEY *comes in* R. *with a decanter of sherry. The other two break apart. She puts the sherry on the table* R.C.)

MRS. LINLEY. Have you been renewing your acquaintance?

MATTHEWS. Very pleasantly, Ma'am.

MRS. LINLEY (*crossing down* L. *and up* C. *again*). Charming! I can't find the key of the china cabinet. Have you got it, Elizabeth?

ELIZABETH (L. *of harpsichord, in a strangled voice*). It's here, Mama. (*She fetches it from the bureau up* C.)

MRS. LINLEY (*crossing up* C. *and taking the key from* ELIZABETH). I wish you would return a thing when you have finished with it. . . . Captain Matthews wants some tickets for your father's concert, Elizabeth. There they are. (*In a whisper as she passes.*) Be sure to sell him the guinea ones.

(*She goes out* L.)

ELIZABETH (*picking up* POLLY'S *basket*). The tickets are a guinea and half a guinea. How many did you want?

MATTHEWS. As many as you will give me five kisses apiece for.

(*He seizes the basket roughly. They stare at each other across it.*)

ELIZABETH (*horrified*). I will scream and summon my father.

MATTHEWS. No, you won't, my pretty one; no, you won't. I have those letters with me. (*He taps his breast pocket.*)

(*There is a knock at the front door.*)

ELIZABETH (*letting go the basket*). I must answer the door.

MATTHEWS (C., *trying to stop her*). Let the servant go.

ELIZABETH (L.C.). We have no servant. Didn't you hear what Mama said about the key of the china cabinet? That is one of my duties—so is the front door.

(*The knock is repeated.*)

MATTHEWS (*sulkily*). Your mother's economies are ridiculous. You must be rich enough to keep ten servants.

ELIZABETH. Please let me pass.

(*He steps aside.* ELIZABETH *runs out* R. *to the entrance hall.* MATTHEWS *puts the basket on the harpsichord and fumes up and down the room.* POLLY *puts her head through the other door, but seeing him stop to look at her she disappears again quickly. Voices are heard outside, and* ELIZABETH *enters with* SHELAH O'GRADY. *She is the* SHERIDANS' *servant, a stout, good-natured woman of fifty, with a pronounced brogue.*)

Come in, Shelah; come in.

SHELAH (R.). Well, that's a rare welcome to be sure, Miss Linley.

ELIZABETH (*down* R.). I was so glad to see you!

(MATTHEWS *gives* SHELAH *one disgusted look, then turning his back he picks up a book from the harpsichord and retires to the window with it.*)

SHELAH. You look pale, me darlin'. You should drink goats' whey. (*In a loud whisper*, R.) Who's the grand military gentleman?

ELIZABETH (*with reserve*). Captain Matthews.

SHELAH. Him that plays whist?

ELIZABETH. Yes.

SHELAH (*giving him a look*). Ah! He travels without his wife, I hear. Never trust that sort, Miss Linley.

ELIZABETH. I don't.

SHELAH (*sighing*). I was nearly had that way meself once. Seven children he had when all was known. Glory be—and he had the grandest pair of blue eyes on him that ye ever saw on anyone! But his heart was black. Ah, it's mighty careful we women have to be, Miss Linley, because very few of them are to be trusted—very few indeed.

ELIZABETH. I will tell Alicia you are here.

(*She goes towards the other door* L. MATTHEWS *at once rushes to her.*)

MATTHEWS (*urgently*). I must speak to you alone.

(SHELAH *stares at them.*)

ELIZABETH. Be quiet. She'll hear you!

SHELAH. No, I'm deaf.

(SHELAH *and* MATTHEWS *glare at each other.* ELIZABETH *runs out, almost colliding with* MRS. LINLEY, *who is returning with a trayful of glasses.*)

MRS. LINLEY. Elizabeth! You nearly knocked me down. (*She puts the glasses on the table up* R., *then distantly.*) So you have come at last, Mrs. O'Grady. Miss Sheridan has a toothache.

SHELAH (R.). Didn't I want to take her to a toothdrawer last night? But would she go? Not she!

B

I'll have to tell Master Richard. She'll do anything for him.

(ELIZABETH *and* ALICIA *come in* L. ALICIA *has a small bottle in her hand.*)

ALICIA (L.). You're late, Shelah. (*She sees* MATTHEWS *and stops.*) Oh!

MRS. LINLEY. This is Miss Sheridan, Captain Matthews.

MATTHEWS (*coldly*). Your servant, ma'am. (*He turns his back.*)

(ALICIA *rises in the middle of a curtsy and stares at him.*)

SHELAH (*crossing* L.C.). They kept me waiting at the circulating library until the feet nearly dropped off me.

ALICIA (L.). Did you get the books I wanted?

SHELAH. I did, then, though I had to snap "Mistakes of the Heart" from under the very nose of Lady Wilmott.

(*She holds out three books so that* ALICIA *and* ELIZABETH *can read the titles.* ALICIA *takes the books.*)

ELIZABETH. "The Delicate Distress." I want to read that one. Will you lend it to me before you return it, Alicia?

ALICIA. Yes. I will have finished it to-morrow.

SHELAH. I never knew such children for books. The whole three of them would read their eyes out of their heads if I'd let them.

MRS. LINLEY (*crossing to* R.C.). It is a pity they have nothing better to do. In my opinion a circulating library is an evergreen tree of diabolical knowledge. "Delicate Distress," indeed! And where do you think you are going to find the time to read rubbishy books, Elizabeth, with your father's benefit concert coming off next week?

SHELAH (C.). If she rehearses all that time, sure won't the throat go back on her, Mrs. Linley! A nice little romance to read is just what will do her good. (*She sighs.*) I've a great liking for romance meself.

MRS. LINLEY (*above the settee—coldly*). Indeed?
SHELAH (*taking the hint*). It is time we were going, Miss Alicia. (*Crossing* R.) We mustn't outstay our welcome. Is your cloak in the hall? (*She opens the door.*)
ALICIA (*following*). Yes.
ELIZABETH (*kindly, moving up* R.). I hope your toothache will be better to-morrow.
ALICIA. I was nearly forgetting the laudanum! (*She holds out the bottle to* ELIZABETH.) Here it is. It has stopped the pain.
ELIZABETH. But you will go to the dentist all the same, won't you?
SHELAH. Master Richard will take her this very day.

(*They are near the door.*)

ALICIA (*turning to* MRS. LINLEY). Good day, ma'am.
MRS. LINLEY. Good day.

(ALICIA *looks at* MATTHEWS, *who takes no notice. She pulls a little face at his back.* ALICIA, SHELAH *and* ELIZABETH *go out into the hall.* MRS. LINLEY *brings two glasses to the table and begins pouring out the wine. The outer door bangs.*)

MRS. LINLEY. I like my servants to keep their place. That woman does not know hers.
MATTHEWS. I agree, she does not.
MRS. LINLEY. Your glass, Captain Matthews.

(ELIZABETH *comes back* R.)

MATTHEWS (*taking it*). Will you not partake also, Miss Linley?
ELIZABETH. No, thank you.
MRS. LINLEY (*up* C.). Elizabeth is too young to drink wine in the middle of the morning.
MATTHEWS (L.C., *raising his glass*). Here's a toast. To the lovely lady of the house.

(*He drinks.* ELIZABETH *turns quickly to the window up* R.C.)

MRS. LINLEY. Oh, Captain Matthews! I'm forty!
MATTHEWS (*swiftly*). Madam, you are no older than you look.
MRS. LINLEY. You're a bad, wicked flatterer, sir. I don't know what Mr. Linley would say if he heard you.

(*There is another knock outside.*)

Now, who can that be?

ELIZABETH (*looking out of the window*). It looks like Mr. Sheridan——

MRS. LINLEY. That man!

(*Another knock.*)

Well, I suppose I shall have to admit him. (*She puts her glass on the table* R.C.) You can just find your father, Elizabeth; I refuse to try to be polite to him alone.

(*She goes out to the hall.* ELIZABETH *turns to run out of the other door.* MATTHEWS *seizes her in his arms as she passes him and kisses her full on the lips.* ELIZABETH *breaks away from him immediately.*)

ELIZABETH (*panting*). Oh! You — you odious wretch!

(*He laughs and tries to kiss her again. Swiftly and instinctively she slaps his face; then filled with shame and surprise drops her hand.*)

MATTHEWS (*angrily*). You'll pay for that, you little fury.

(*They stand staring at each other for a moment, so that* RICHARD, *opening the door for his hostess, sees them.* ELIZABETH *at once turns and goes swiftly out.* RICHARD *steps back against the door to allow* MRS. LINLEY *to enter. She is followed by* THOMAS SHERIDAN *and* CHARLES. RICHARD *closes the door and comes into the room.*

THOMAS SHERIDAN *is a short, pompous gentleman of fifty. His more formal speech proclaims that he is an actor and would-be orator, but when he is excited he is apt to revert to his natural brogue.*

CHARLES *is a self-possessed young man of twenty-two, with an intelligent and somewhat cynical expression. He is fairer than the rest of the family and he carries himself more elegantly. Although something of a prig, he is endowed with a shrewd mind and admirable common sense. He is rather attractive on this account.*

RICHARD *is twenty-one, tall and slender and restlessly alive. He has dark, wavy hair, brilliant grey eyes, and a tongue that is never still. His good humour is irrepressible, and he is inclined to treat everything in life with the utmost levity; but his passions are easily aroused and just now he is angry with* MATTHEWS, *who appears completely indifferent to his baleful glances. His charm can be sensed at once; his genius is totally unsuspected.*)

MRS. LINLEY (*crossing up* C.). This is Mr. Sheridan, Captain Matthews.

MATTHEWS (L.C., *insolently*). The play actor, I presume?

SHERIDAN (*moving up* R.C.). I would prefer to describe myself more simply, sir, as Thomas Sheridan—gentleman.

RICHARD (R.). Landed gentleman and descendant of the kings of Cavan—— You forgot the rest of it, Father.

CHARLES (*above the settee*). Don't be absurd, Richard.

SHERIDAN. These are my two sons, Charles and Richard.

(*They all bow to each other. There is a pause.*)

MRS. LINLEY. We may as well sit.

(SHERIDAN *and* RICHARD *sit on the settee;* CHARLES *down* R. MATTHEWS *brings the chair from up* R.C. *to* L. *of the table* R.C. *for* MRS. LINLEY, *then brings one over from down* L. *to* L.C. *for himself. There is another pause, during which* SHERIDAN *eyes the wine-glass meaningly.*)

Er—will you have some sherry, Mr. Sheridan? (*She brings glasses from the table up* C.)

SHERIDAN. Ah, thank you! My favourite wine! Sherry for Sherry, as my father always said.

(MRS. LINLEY *very grudgingly pours out three small glassfuls for the* SHERIDANS, *then refills her own and* MATTHEWS' *generously.* CHARLES *and* RICHARD *exchange eloquent glances.*)

RICHARD. Any sort of wine suits *this* Sheridan.
CHARLES. A statement that shows you have no discrimination.

(MRS. LINLEY *gives glasses to* SHERIDAN, *which he passes over* R., *then gives one to* MATTHEWS, *then keeps one for himself.*)

SHERIDAN (*raising his glass*). Here's to healths, hearts and homes!

(*All rise and bow.*)

RICHARD (*boisterously*). Hearts especially!

(MRS. LINLEY *looks at him with extreme dislike.*)

MATTHEWS (*sententiously*). Homes! (*He bows to* MRS. LINLEY.) And Whist!

(*All drink and sit again.*)

MRS. LINLEY (*smiling at him*). Captain Matthews is the most elegant whist player in Bath, Mr. Sheridan.

SHERIDAN. Indeed? I don't care for card games myself, and whist has always seemed to me the last resource of the unintelligent. I prefer to seek my recreation among the poets, ma'am, particularly in the company of our greatest bard—the immortal Swan of Avon.

RICHARD (*piously*). Shakespeare, you know.
MRS. LINLEY. I'm not quite a fool, Mr. Richard.

(MR. LINLEY *and* ELIZABETH *come in* L. *The men jump to their feet.*)

SHERIDAN. Good morning, Mr. Linley. You know my sons?

LINLEY (L.). Good morning, good morning. Yes, I've seen them about Bath.

CHARLES (*down* R.). Good morning, Miss Linley.

RICHARD (R.). You did not visit the Pump Room this morning, Miss Linley. Every man in Bath was disappointed.

ELIZABETH (*indifferently*). I was practising my songs for the concert.

(LINLEY *has noticed the visitors are drinking his wine.*)

LINLEY (*dryly*). I trust you approve my wine, Mr. Sheridan?

SHERIDAN (*unenthusiastically*). It is quite tolerably good, sir.

LINLEY. Indeed?

SHERIDAN (*looking into his empty glass*). Will you not join us in a toast?

LINLEY. Thank you, but I never drink at this time of day.

RICHARD. The Sheridans drink whenever they can.

CHARLES. Richard! You will be misunderstood!

SHERIDAN (R.C., *putting down his glass*). Well, I expect you are wondering to what you owe this intrusion.

LINLEY. Not at all, not at all. I presume you have come to settle your account for Miss Sheridan's singing lessons.

SHERIDAN (R.C., *uncomfortably*). Er—no, not exactly. Though of course in due time—— (*He glances meaningly at* MATTHEWS.) The matter was purely domestic.

MATTHEWS. With your permission, Mrs. Linley, I will take my leave. We shall meet at the Colonel's reception to-morrow evening. You have received your invitation, I trust?

MRS. LINLEY (*rising*). This very morning.

MATTHEWS. Perhaps you will allow me to escort you and Miss Linley in my carriage.

MRS. LINLEY. You may call for Mr. Linley and me. I have refused the Colonel's invitation on Elizabeth's behalf. She is much too busy at present.

MATTHEWS. But, Mrs. Linley——

ELIZABETH (*down* L.). Neither would I care to go even if you had accepted for me, Mama.

MRS. LINLEY. I disapprove of these new hoity-toity ways of yours, Elizabeth. (*Stepping* L.C.) I don't know what the Captain will think of you.

(ELIZABETH *looks away, humiliated.*)

LINLEY (L., *coming to her rescue*). If Elizabeth is to be a great musician, Mrs. Linley, she is wise to refuse invitations to card parties. Moreover, I think she is old enough to decide for herself in the future.

MRS. LINLEY (L.C.). I shall have something to say to that, Mr. Linley. If you must go, Captain Matthews, I will show you out. (*She crosses above to* R.)

MATTHEWS (C., *bowing*). Good morning! (*As he goes out with* MRS. LINLEY.) As partners we should be invincible. I venture to think we could safely challenge any other pair in Bath——

(*They go out* R.)

SHERIDAN (R.C.). Not a very friendly sort of person, is he? (*He sits on the settee.*)

CHARLES (*down* R.). He comes of a very good Welsh family, I believe. His manners are certainly distinguished.

RICHARD (C., *hotly*). His manners are most insolent, and whatever his family is, it can't be any older, or more honourable, than ours.

(ELIZABETH *brings chair from* L.C. *to down* L. *and sits.*)

SHERIDAN. Impossible!

RICHARD. I took a dislike to him the first moment I saw him.

LINLEY (*mildly*). You appear to be a very intolerant young man, Mr. Richard.

RICHARD. Am I misjudging him, Miss Linley?

ELIZABETH (*in a low voice*). How could I know, Mr. Sheridan?

(MRS. LINLEY *comes back radiant.* SHERIDAN *rises.*)

MRS. LINLEY (*to below settee*). What a charming man! Such a flatterer—though I believe he is sincere in his compliments. His wife doesn't deserve him.

LINLEY (L.). I do not recollect that you have ever met his wife, Mrs. Linley.

MRS. LINLEY (*crossing* L.C.). No, but I am quite sure she is unworthy of him. Has Mr. Sheridan told you his business?

LINLEY. Not yet.

SHERIDAN (R.C.). It partly concerns you, ma'am.

MRS. LINLEY (L.C.). Me! (*She looks quickly at her husband.*) Let me assure you, Mr. Sheridan, my husband has no money to lend, so it is no use asking me to influence him.

(RICHARD *works down* R. *of settee.*)

ELIZABETH (*down* L., *in a horrified whisper*). Mama!

MRS. LINLEY. Be quiet, Elizabeth. I know the Sheridans' reputation in Bath, even if you do not.

SHERIDAN. Madam, I did not come to ask for monetary favours, but merely to beg kindness for my motherless girl. I came because you are the only lady in Bath who once knew my poor dear wife, and because you, too, have daughters of your own. I see I was mistaken. We will retire—— (*He signals to his sons to follow suit.*) Good day, ma'am.

MRS. LINLEY (*crossing* R.C.). Now, Mr. Sheridan, don't take on so. I spoke in haste. I have a quick nature. Mr. Linley, do I not frequently speak in haste?

LINLEY (L.). Frequently, my dear, very frequently.

MRS. LINLEY (R.C.). Please state your request, Mr. Sheridan, and I shall be only too willing to help you—if it is reasonable, of course.

(SHERIDAN *and* MRS. LINLEY *sit on the settee.*)

SHERIDAN. This morning, by the mail-coach, I received from Dublin an urgent request to revisit the theatre there. The manager was kind enough to say that for too long had the Irish people been deprived of the talent of their greatest Roscius.

Mrs. Linley. Did he mean *you*?

Sheridan. Yes! Mistaken though he may have been, he meant—me. I would, myself, prefer to remain in Bath. The art of oratory and pronunciation is very dear to me. My Academy of Elocution here is just beginning to make its influence felt. (*Rising and crossing* c.) Did I tell you that the young Marquis of Buckingham is one of my pupils?

Linley (*wearily*). I believe you did—once or twice.

Sheridan (c.). But the times are so depressed, and elocution, if I may say so, is not yet considered one of the actual necessities of life. My financial position——

Linley (*hastily*). I understand. So you feel obliged to accept this Dublin offer.

Sheridan. Obliged! Thank you, that is precisely the word. For the sake of my children I feel obliged to accept. I must start to-morrow morning.

Mrs. Linley. But what did you wish me to do?

Sheridan (*holding up his hand*). I am coming to that. My financial position is such that it does not permit of my taking my family to Dublin with me. They must remain here in our modest apartments, until my return next winter. My daughter will therefore be left entirely without her natural protectors——

Richard (*down* r.). What about Charles and me?

Sheridan. Left, I say, without her natural protectors. This is my request. Will you, Mrs. Linley, be a mother to her? (*Moving down* l.) Will you, Miss Linley, be her sister as well as her friend?

Elizabeth. Alicia is already almost as dear to me as my sisters.

Sheridan (*to* c. *again*). And you, Mrs. Linley?

Mrs. Linley (*rising* r.c.). Of course, I will act as her duenna at the Assembly Rooms—if that is what you mean—though, poor girl, I think her chances of a good match are very small.

(Linley *moves up* c.)

Sheridan. But will you cherish her, Mrs. Linley, will you watch over her as over your own dear daughters?

MRS. LINLEY. Well—er—really, Mr. Sheridan—I——

SHERIDAN. I thank you, ma'am. I thank you from the bottom of a father's heart. (*He shakes her hand.*)

LINLEY (*moving to above the settee*). But what are these two young gentlemen going to do during your absence? I can foresee that they will soon get into mischief if they are allowed to remain idle in Bath.

CHARLES (*moving to* L. *of settee*). You misjudge us, sir. I think our father can trust us. I am exceedingly employed studying for a post in the Diplomatic Service.

SHERIDAN (*to below table* R.C.). Charles is of a very studious and sedentary disposition, and I have always felt his talents would show to advantage in Diplomacy.

LINLEY (*above settee*). And what about this other young man? What profession is he preparing for?

RICHARD (*moving to* R. *of the settee*). To tell the truth at the present—none. My talents, for the moment, might be described as disengaged. That's an idea, Father! I might walk through the streets of Bath every morning with a notice on my brow saying "To Let."

SHERIDAN. And underneath you can write "Unfurnished."

(LINLEY *moves down* R. *of settee.*)

RICHARD. Well, Henry Angelo has taught me some skill with the foils. I could be a fencing master.

CHARLES. Even that would be better than scribbling for a living!

SHERIDAN. Richard is destined for the Bar, Mr. Linley.

ELIZABETH (*kindly*). A most respectable calling, Mr. Sheridan.

MRS. LINLEY (L.). Almost too respectable.

RICHARD (*crossing to* L.C.). When Richard Brinsley Sheridan is called to the Bar, ma'am, the rest of the faculty may look to their laurels, for I was born to be famous. It is written in the stars.

SHERIDAN (R.C.). Who said so?

RICHARD (*solemnly*). Shelah.
MRS. LINLEY (L.C.). Mrs. O'Grady?
ELIZABETH (*rising*). She has second sight, Mama. She tells fortunes in teacups. (*She moves up* L.C.)
MRS. LINLEY (*eagerly*). Why didn't you tell me before? She shall tell mine the very next time she comes.
LINLEY (R.). If a ready tongue is all a lawyer needs, I think you will be famous, Mr. Richard.
RICHARD. Thank you, sir. You fill me with hope.

(POLLY *looks in* L. *and crosses to* C.)

POLLY. Mama, you had better come—— (*Joyously.*) Dick! And I thought it was only that horrid Captain Matthews who was here.
RICHARD. My dear love!

(*He picks her up in his arms and kisses her heartily. She throws her arms round his neck, hugging him. He then puts* POLLY *over to his* R.)

LINLEY. Where are your manners, Polly? I don't know what Mr. Sheridan will think.
MRS. LINLEY. And she wouldn't kiss the Captain when I told her to, the bad, wicked girl!
POLLY (*remembering*). Something is burning in the kitchen, Mama!
MRS. LINLEY. My dinner——

(*She bustles out* L.)

LINLEY (R.). If you will excuse me too, Mr. Sheridan, I must see to Tom's practising.
SHERIDAN. Of course, of course. We must not keep you. Good day, sir.
LINLEY. I will see you to the door.
SHERIDAN. Please don't trouble.
LINLEY. Not at all, a pleasure——

(SHERIDAN *and* LINLEY *go out* R. CHARLES *hesitates a moment.*)

CHARLES. Good day, Miss Linley. I trust we shall meet again to-morrow.
ELIZABETH (L.). I am always glad to meet—friends.

(CHARLES *bows and goes out.*)

RICHARD (*to* POLLY). I'll have to go too.

POLLY (R.C.). And I've only seen you for half a minute.

RICHARD (C., *kissing her hand*). Never mind, remember I love you all the same.

POLLY. Best in the world?

RICHARD. Best in the world—except one.

POLLY. Who is that?

ELIZABETH (*smiling*). His sister, of course.

RICHARD (C.). No. Someone else's sister.

CHARLES (*outside*). Richard!

POLLY. Who is she?

RICHARD (*kissing* ELIZABETH'S *hand*). Guess!

POLLY (*understanding*). Oh!

RICHARD (*laughing at her as he crosses* R.). Good-bye.

(*He goes out* R.)

POLLY. Isn't he wonderful?

(*She runs to the window* R.C. *to look after him.* LINLEY *returns from the hall.*)

LINLEY. Dear, dear, the whole morning wasted.

(*He goes out through the other door* L. ELIZABETH *moves towards the window* L.C.)

POLLY (*looking after him still*). I like Richard better than anyone else in the world—except you and Papa and Mama, of course.

ELIZABETH (*teasing her*). That is very generous of you, Polly.

POLLY. Why?

ELIZABETH (*crossing up* R.C.). If I were you, I should hate to be told I was only second best.

POLLY (*up* C., *simply*). But you're the eldest.

ELIZABETH. Me! (*She suddenly understands.*) Oh—me! (*She stands looking at the door, smiling with amusement.*)

CURTAIN.

Scene 2

SCENE.—*The same; the following evening.* MR. LINLEY, *wearing his best clothes, is sitting calmly by his harpsichord reading a music manuscript.* MRS. LINLEY *comes in* L., *very fussy and excited, dressed for the reception. The room looks vaguely untidy. The table which was* R.C. *in Scene 1 is now against the wall down* R. *and is covered with music. A stool is* L. *of it.*

MRS. LINLEY (*crossing up* C.). Dear me! Captain Matthews is very late. (*She goes to the window* R.C. *and looks out through the shutters.*) Not a sign of him yet. I wonder if he has forgotten to call for us? (*She turns to* LINLEY.)

LINLEY (*indifferently*). Very likely.

MRS. LINLEY (*moving to above harpsichord*). We'll give him another ten minutes, then we'll have to order a hackney coach, in spite of the expense. You know how annoyed the Colonel becomes when guests are late. Do you think—— You're not paying the slightest attention to me, Mr. Linley.

LINLEY (*looking up*). Eh?

MRS. LINLEY. I think you find your best pleasure in tantalizing me, Mr. Linley!

(*He drops his head over his score again.*)

I believe you don't *want* to go to the reception.

LINLEY. Quite true, my dear.

MRS. LINLEY (*crossing* R.C.). And is this what I get for slaving my fingers to the bone angling to have us sent an invitation? You're not worthy of my anxiety on your behalf, Mr. Linley. You simply don't *wish* to cut a figure in society. (*She moves up* R. *of settee to* C.) I wonder why I ever married you!

LINLEY. I often wonder that, too.

MRS. LINLEY (C.). Ten children is all I ever got out of marriage—and then to hear every day of my life that they get all their talents and their good looks from *you.*

(LINLEY *takes no notice. She draws her finger along the table up* R.)

Just look at this room. It's like a pigsty. Where are those girls? (*She crosses down* L. *and shouts into the inner room.*) Polly! Elizabeth!
  POLLY (*outside*). Yes, Mama.
  MRS. LINLEY. Come here.

(POLLY *comes in.*)

Were you copying that music? (*She moves* R.C.)
  POLLY. No, Mama. That belongs to Elizabeth. I did the dusting——
  MRS. LINLEY (*moving up* R.C.). Dusting! Look at this table. Do you call that dusted?
  POLLY (*up* L.C.). I hadn't got that far, Mama.
  MRS. LINLEY. In my young days we never dreamt of leaving a task half done.
  POLLY (*up* C.). But you called me away to give the twins their milk.
  MRS. LINLEY. Nonsense! You should have done it this morning.
  POLLY. But, Mama, this morning you sent me to the Assembly Rooms—to sell tickets for Papa's benefit concert.
  MRS. LINLEY (*up* R.C.). That is enough. The fact remains that the table hasn't been touched since yesterday. This bottle has been here since that wretched girl used it. (*She picks it up.*) Get your duster and begin.

(POLLY *takes a duster from under a cushion on the window seat and begins.* ELIZABETH *comes in* L.)

  ELIZABETH (*coming* L.C.). Did you want me, Mama?
  MRS. LINLEY. When you lend my laudanum to friends, Elizabeth, you might at least be kind enough to return it to its proper place.
  ELIZABETH (*taking it*). Yes, Mama. (*She crosses* L.)
  MRS. LINLEY. Is that your music?
  ELIZABETH (*wearily*). Yes, Mama.
  MRS. LINLEY. Then see that it is all tidied away before you retire.

(ELIZABETH *puts down the bottle on top of the music on the table down* R.)

Have you put the children to bed?

ELIZABETH. All except Tom and Maria.

MRS. LINLEY. Then you may as well go on with your copying.

(ELIZABETH *sits at the table down* R. *and takes up her pen.*)

Dear, dear, I wish that man would hasten.

(LINLEY *raises his hand, listening.* ELIZABETH *reaches for another candle.*)

(*Moving down* C.) One candle is enough, Elizabeth. Your father is not *made* of money.

LINLEY (*rising*). I would rather that she used two candles than strained her eyes. The coach is coming, I think . . .

MRS. LINLEY. What ears you have to be sure! (*She rushes to the window* R.C.) Yes, here it is.

LINLEY. I will get my coat.

(*He goes into the inner room* L.)

MRS. LINLEY. Open the door for the Captain, Polly.

(POLLY *hesitates.* ELIZABETH *rises.*)

Where are you going, Elizabeth?

ELIZABETH (*crossing* L.). Only to the other room, Mama.

MRS. LINLEY. You will stay here and be polite to the Captain.

ELIZABETH (L.). Please let me go, Mama.

MRS. LINLEY. What is the matter, Elizabeth?

(ELIZABETH *turns away.*)

There is something going on that I don't understand. Both you and Polly are behaving most unbecomingly. You will kindly explain yourself. Polly! Go at once and open the door for the Captain.

(POLLY *goes out reluctantly,* R.)

ELIZABETH. I do not wish to meet Captain Matthews again.
MRS. LINLEY (*amazed*). Pray why not?
ELIZABETH. He... he... I think... I mean —he——
MRS. LINLEY (L.C., *magnificently*). Well?
ELIZABETH (L., *in a rush*). I'm afraid he is in love with me.
MRS. LINLEY. What! In love with you! Nonsense! Your head has been completely turned by the compliments of a few schoolboys as foolish as that young Richard Sheridan.
ELIZABETH. But, Mama...
MRS. LINLEY. Do you think because you have a pretty face, and can bawl a few ballads, that a gentleman of Captain Matthews' experience would take any notice of you? Why, you're nothing but a child.
ELIZABETH. I wish I were.
MRS. LINLEY. As a matter of fact, I happen to know why Captain Matthews comes here so often. But it is not to see *you*, make no mistake about *that*. He naturally prefers a woman of—well, presence. It is all perfectly correct, of course, and no harm to your father. He's married too. (*With a sigh.*) Nothing becomes a man like regimentals. Sometimes I wish your poor father was more imposing.

(POLLY *opens the door from the hall and* ELIZABETH *turns to flee, almost colliding with* LINLEY, *who is entering from the inner room.* POLLY *is followed by* EDWARD KNIGHT, *a gay, handsome lad in uniform. His bright eyes dart about the room.*)

MRS. LINLEY. Really, Elizabeth, I wish you would remember you're not a child any longer.
KNIGHT. Mrs. Linley?

(*Hearing the strange voice,* ELIZABETH *turns, and in her relief, smiles at him.*)

MRS. LINLEY (C.). Yes! This is Mr. Linley.
KNIGHT (*above the settee*). Captain Edward Knight,

your servant, ma'am, your servant, sir. My friend and kinsman, Captain Matthews, sends his compliments, and will you allow me to escort you in his coach to the reception, as he has been unavoidably delayed. He hopes to follow us later.

LINLEY (L.C.). And what will the Colonel say to that?

KNIGHT. Captain Matthews has already despatched a letter of explanation, sir.

LINLEY. I see. Well, we shall be needing to despatch one ourselves if we don't hurry.

(KNIGHT *is staring at* ELIZABETH, *who is down* L. POLLY *is down* R.)

KNIGHT. Miss Linley, I presume?

MRS. LINLEY. They are both my daughters.

KNIGHT (*gallantly*). So at last I meet the famous Maid of Bath!! (*Bowing.*) Your—your *slave*, ma'am.

(ELIZABETH *cannot help smiling.*)

MRS. LINLEY (*crossing to door* R.). Come, come, Captain, we must hasten. You will doubtless have other opportunities of paying compliments to Elizabeth.

KNIGHT. Elizabeth! Divine name!

(LINLEY *frowns impatiently.*)

MRS. LINLEY (*glancing at* ELIZABETH *severely*). It's enough to turn any girl's head—— Come, Captain.

(*She sweeps out* R.)

LINLEY (*as* KNIGHT *steps aside for him*). After *you*, sir.

(KNIGHT *goes out unwillingly.* LINLEY *turns back to* ELIZABETH *and speaks with almost reluctant fondness.*)

Don't sit up too late over that copying, Elizabeth.

ELIZABETH (L., *smiling*). No, Papa.

(LINLEY *goes out* R.)

POLLY. Captain Knight is much pleasanter than his cousin, isn't he, Elizabeth?

ELIZABETH. Very much.

(*The door bangs downstairs.* ELIZABETH *blows out the candle on the harpsichord.*)

POLLY (*coming to* ELIZABETH). All the gentlemen fall in love with you, Elizabeth, the moment they see you.

ELIZABETH (*bitterly*). That's not love.

POLLY. Isn't it?

ELIZABETH. You'll know soon enough yourself, Polly. We are public performers. Men think they have only to ask and we will be honoured to give.

POLLY (R.C.). Give what?

ELIZABETH. Kisses and things.

POLLY. Captain Matthews wanted *me* to kiss him yesterday.

ELIZABETH. Captain Matthews!

POLLY. Yes—and he looked so strangely at me . . . But I wouldn't. That is why Mama was so angry when I kissed Dick.

ELIZABETH. The villain! Listen, Polly. If ever any other gentleman asks you, you must say no, and tell me. Promise!

POLLY. Except Dick——?

ELIZABETH (*laughing*). Oh, I think poor Mr. Sheridan is to be trusted. Promise!

POLLY. Very well.

(*There is a knock at the front door.*)

ELIZABETH. That will be Alicia with the library book.

(POLLY *runs out.* ELIZABETH *looks swiftly round the room, hiding* POLLY'S *duster and tidying the music. The door bangs outside.* POLLY *runs in again. She is very frightened, and clings to* ELIZABETH.)

POLLY. I tried to stop him, but he pushed the door open.

ELIZABETH (L.). Who?

(MATTHEWS *comes in. The two girls stare at him in terror.*)

POLLY. Him!

ELIZABETH (*keeping her voice steady*). I presume you called for my parents. They are already gone.

MATTHEWS. I came to speak to *you*—alone.

ELIZABETH. But I do not wish to speak with you, Captain Matthews.

MATTHEWS (*coming a step nearer*). I have no time to waste. Send that child out of the room.

POLLY (*terrified*). Elizabeth!

ELIZABETH (*proudly*). Since you have yourself contrived that our parents should be gone when you called, I need not remind you that Polly and I are unprotected and defenceless.

MATTHEWS (*roughly*). I mean you no harm, but I must see you—and alone. I cannot stay more than a few moments. Polly must go away. (*He crosses down L. and opens the door.*)

POLLY. I won't.

MATTHEWS (*down L., dangerously*). You will, I think. Or do you prefer that I say what I have to say in front of her, Elizabeth?

ELIZABETH. No. Go into the next room for a few moments, Polly.

POLLY. But——

ELIZABETH. Please! I'll call out if I want you.

POLLY (*reluctantly*). I'll stand just inside the door.

ELIZABETH (C.). Yes, dear. But shut it first.

(POLLY *goes out into the inner room* L.)

Now, sir, I am ready to receive your insults.

MATTHEWS (*coming to her*, L.C.). Elizabeth, my love. (*He seizes her hand.*) Don't you know that I could not force myself upon you like this were I not distracted?

ELIZABETH (C.). You are indeed distracted.

MATTHEWS (*ardently*). I love you, Elizabeth, and so much that I will stop at no obstacle to win you.

ELIZABETH. Win me! You are not free to win any woman. You are already married.

MATTHEWS. I am not talking of marriage. I am speaking of *love*.

ELIZABETH (*moving* R.). Love and marriage mean the same thing to *me*, Captain Matthews.

MATTHEWS (*following to* R.C.—*getting angry*). These ladylike airs and graces may hoodwink boys, Elizabeth, but they don't deceive me. You may be the loveliest girl in Bath, and the sweetest singer in England, but you *are* a singer, and all the talents you possess cannot make you otherwise.

ELIZABETH (*moving up* R.). Indeed, sir! Then let a mere singer order you out of her house!

MATTHEWS (C.). Bravo! An actress too! You should join forces with your pompous friend Mr. Sheridan, and play Shakespeare with his jackanapes of sons.

ELIZABETH (*coming to above settee*). Please make an end of your insults. What do you want of me?

MATTHEWS. Your love—— (*He drops his voice.*) Yourself.

ELIZABETH (*horrified*). Myself!

MATTHEWS (*eagerly, stepping to* L. *of her*). I have planned it all out. To-morrow night your father will be rehearsing the orchestra for the Lenten concerts in the Assembly Rooms, and I happen to know your mother is playing cards at Lady Wilmott's. You will plead a headache, and so will be excused attendance at the rehearsal. At eight o'clock I will be in the summerhouse where we met last summer. You will join me there. No one will miss you, and you can be back before eleven. We can arrange then how we are to meet in the future.

ELIZABETH. Is there no end to your baseness?

MATTHEWS. You will be there, my pretty.

ELIZABETH. I may be a public singer, Captain Matthews, but my favours cannot be bought.

MATTHEWS (*lightly*). No? (*Then darkly.*) Not even if I tell you I will shoot myself on your doorstep if you refuse?

ELIZABETH (*recoiling*). Oh! (*She backs and sits on the stool down* R.)

MATTHEWS (*following her down* R. *of settee*). Not even if I tell you that before I shoot myself a certain packet of letters will be delivered into your father's keeping, and a certain paragraph posted in the Bath newspapers?

ELIZABETH. What shall I do? What shall I do?

MATTHEWS. Meet me in the garden, and the letters will be yours to-morrow evening.

ELIZABETH (*rising to* L. *of him*). You mean that I must part with my virtue as the price of last summer's foolishness? No! I'll confess to my father! (*She goes* C.)

MATTHEWS (R.C., *taking out a letter*). How did that last one go? "Good-bye, my dearest, dearest Captain. Betsy will think of you every day."

(ELIZABETH *tries to snatch it*.)

Not so fast, my lady, not so fast.

(ELIZABETH *throws herself on the harpsichord stool sobbing.* MATTHEWS *follows her*.)

You'll come to the garden, pretty one?

ELIZABETH. I must think.

MATTHEWS. You'll come to the garden?

ELIZABETH. Yes—yes, I'll come.

MATTHEWS (*picking up her hand*). I thought you would be sensible in the end.

ELIZABETH (*snatching her hand away*). Sensible!

MATTHEWS (*bending over her and kissing her*). Until to-morrow, then, my love.

(ELIZABETH *breaks away*.)

(*He bows ironically*.) Your devoted—lover, ma'am.

(*He goes out* R. ELIZABETH *paces the room beating her hands. The outside door bangs softly. She returns to her seat before the table and takes up her pen. Her eyes fall on the bottle of laudanum. She puts down her pen slowly; still gazing at it, then with a gesture of despair, she rises, takes out the cork, and drinks the entire contents of the bottle. Dropping it out of her hand on to the table again, she puts her hand to her heart and staggers backwards, then falls on to the settee, staring in front of her.* POLLY *opens the door an inch.*)

POLLY (*whispering*). Elizabeth! Has he gone?

(ELIZABETH *does not reply.* POLLY *opens the door wider and looks in. Seeing* ELIZABETH'S *strange expression, she becomes frightened.*)

POLLY. Elizabeth! What is the matter? (*She comes to* L. *of the settee.*)

ELIZABETH (*slowly*). I've drunk Mama's laudanum. I'm going to die.

POLLY (*wildly*). Elizabeth!

(ELIZABETH *falls back and closes her eyes. There is a knock outside.*)

Oh, that will be Captain Matthews again!

ELIZABETH (*without opening her eyes*). Let him come upstairs. Let him see me dead.

POLLY (*crying*). Oh! I'm going to look for Papa!

(*She runs out into the hall.* ELIZABETH *sits up slightly, opens her eyes and gingerly feels her heart to find out if it is still beating. She pulls a disgusted face as if she did not care for the taste in her mouth. There are voices and urgent steps outside. She falls back into her original position. The door bursts open. It is* RICHARD. *He is distracted. He runs to her side and, kneeling beside her, puts his ear to her heart. She opens her eyes with a start over his bent head.* POLLY *and* ALICIA *come in,* ALICIA *trying to comfort her. She is carrying a library book, which she puts down on the table.*)

RICHARD (*kneeling* R. *of* ELIZABETH). It's all right, her heart is still beating.

ALICIA (*down* R.). Look! Here is the bottle of

laudanum she lent me yesterday before I had my tooth out. She must have taken all that was left.

RICHARD (*rising and taking it*). It is a very small bottle. How much was in it?

ALICIA. It was about half full——

RICHARD. That's not enough to kill anyone. She has just fainted. (*Crossing* C.) Fetch a bowl, Polly, and we'll dash some water in her face.

POLLY (*eagerly*). Cold water?

ELIZABETH (*involuntarily*). No!

(*The others turn to look at her. She is confused.*)

Where am I?

POLLY (*kneeling* L. *of* ELIZABETH). Oh, you're alive, Elizabeth, you're alive!

ELIZABETH. What is the matter?

ALICIA. You poisoned yourself, you know.

ELIZABETH. I remember now.

RICHARD (C.). But why did you do it, Elizabeth?

(*She looks up at the name.*)

(*Moving to above* L. *of the settee.*) You might have died.

ELIZABETH. I wanted to die.

POLLY. Betsy!

ALICIA (*down* R.). But why?

ELIZABETH. I was frightened——

RICHARD. Who frightened you, my sweet?

(ELIZABETH *starts at the endearment, then drops her eyes.*)

ELIZABETH (*hesitating*). Captain Matthews.

POLLY. I hate him! I hate him!

ALICIA (*warmly*). We all hate him!

RICHARD. He shall not go unchallenged another hour! (*He walks to* L.C.)

ALICIA. But what has he done?

ELIZABETH. He hasn't done anything—yet, I mean. But he asked me—— He insulted me.

RICHARD (L.C.). I shall go straight home for my sword, and then let the wretch look to his safety!

POLLY (*rising to him*). Oh, Dick! You are wonderful.

ALICIA. Richard was designed by nature to be a knight in shining armour.

ELIZABETH. You don't understand, Mr. Sheridan.

RICHARD (*crossing to* R.C.). I imagine it is fairly obvious to understand what manner of insult he offered you.

ALICIA. What did he say, Elizabeth? (*She sits on the stool down* R.)

ELIZABETH. I can't tell anyone that. Oh, I wish I was dead!

RICHARD. Your parents had no right to leave you alone. I will go to the Colonel's house and tell your father—— (*He goes to the door* R.)

ELIZABETH. No! No!

RICHARD. You are hiding something from us, Elizabeth. You must tell us.

ELIZABETH. I can't.

ALICIA. But how can we help you if you don't trust us?

ELIZABETH. I do trust you, Alicia—and Mr. Sheridan.

RICHARD. Then what is it?

(ELIZABETH *hesitates, then suddenly makes up her mind.*)

ELIZABETH. Did you go to see if Tom and Maria were safely in bed, Polly?

POLLY (*reluctantly*). No.

ELIZABETH. Then they may have set their bedclothes on fire by this time for all we know. You had better go and take their candle away.

(ALICIA *gives her a candle from table down* R.)

POLLY (*turning to the door* L. *slowly*). Very well. But you won't go before I come back, will you, Dick?

RICHARD (*crossing to the door* L.). No, ma'am. Until you return, I am rooted here as fast as any evergreen in the garden.

(*He opens the door for her. She goes out.*)

ALICIA. Now, Betsy, tell us everything!

ELIZABETH (*looking shyly at* RICHARD, *then swiftly away*). Captain Matthews has been pestering me with his attentions.

RICHARD. I knew it.

ALICIA. But he's married, isn't he?

ELIZABETH. He did not speak of *marriage*.

RICHARD (L.). The villain! He shall die!

ALICIA. Of course. But do go on, Elizabeth.

ELIZABETH. He came to-night, when he knew Polly and I were alone, meaning to force me to agree to his proposals.

RICHARD. What!

ALICIA. How terrible! What did you say?

ELIZABETH. I said—that is what I am trying to tell you. You see, I was terrified.

RICHARD. Yes, of course you were, you poor child. (*He sits* L. *on the settee.*)

ELIZABETH (*very embarrassed*). The night after to-morrow, Mama will be playing whist at Lady Wilmott's, and Papa will be conducting a rehearsal at the Assembly Rooms. I should be there too, but Captain Matthews told me to pretend I had a headache, and then, when my parents were gone——

RICHARD. Yes?

ELIZABETH. To—to steal away, and meet him in the summer-house at the bottom of the garden. I was horrified!

ALICIA. I'm sure I should have fainted away.

ELIZABETH. I nearly did.

RICHARD. I hope you were not too overcome to tell him that he should pay for his baseness?

ELIZABETH. No.

RICHARD. No?

ELIZABETH. I—I—you see, I was utterly at his mercy.

ALICIA. You don't mean to say that you promised to go?

ELIZABETH (*beginning to cry*). Yes.

ALICIA. Oh, Betsy! But you couldn't.

ELIZABETH. That's why I tried to poison myself.

RICHARD. But why could you not tell your father the whole story ? . . . This is enough to cause Matthews to be hounded out of Bath.

ELIZABETH. He had some letters.

ALICIA. Whose letters ?

ELIZABETH (*faltering*). Mine.

RICHARD (*shattered*). Yours ! (*Rising.*) And I could have prayed to your purity.

ELIZABETH (*earnestly*). Mr. Sheridan, I can't bear to think that you—or Alicia, should think evil of me. It was last summer. I was only a child. I thought it was something grand to have an admirer like every woman of fashion has, writing poems to my voice, and telling me I was the loveliest creature in the world——

ALICIA. Did he ?

ELIZABETH. I did not understand.

(ALICIA *rises and sits at* R. *end of the settee.*)

You do believe me, don't you ?

RICHARD. With all my heart I want to believe you.

ELIZABETH. You believe me, Alicia ?

ALICIA. Yes, I do. I have tried as hard as possible to acquire an admirer myself—meaning to keep him at a respectful distance, of course. A woman simply must have an admirer these days, Richard, for the sake of her own self-respect.

RICHARD (R.C., *passionately*). Then please remember that if anyone attempts to admire either of you in the future, I will run him through !

ALICIA. We're going to live and die old maids, Elizabeth.

ELIZABETH. I can wish for no greater consolation.

RICHARD (*quietly, crossing and sitting on the stool down* R.). Please go on with your story, Elizabeth.

ELIZABETH. I wrote him some foolish letters—you see, I was fond of him then, just as children are fond of those who pet them and take notice of them——

RICHARD (*tormented at the thought of it*). Damnation to him !

Elizabeth. I thought nothing of his—attentions, until the last night before he left Bath——
Richard. Yes——
Elizabeth. We were in the garden—looking at the moon. Then suddenly he threw his arms round me—— (*She shudders and puts her hands over her face.*)
Alicia. Did he kiss you passionately all over your face?
Richard. You have been reading too many library books, Alicia.
Elizabeth. He tried—but I succeeded in evading him.
Alicia. How? He looks excessively strong.
Elizabeth (*tragically*). I bit him.
Alicia. Oh!
Richard. The best thing you could possibly have done.
Elizabeth. He sent me a note next day, saying that I should live to regret it, but when I did not hear from him again I thought he had forgotten—until yesterday. He thinks I am resisting only to encourage him. I am a public singer and should therefore be honoured by his favour. (*Rising and crossing* L.C.) I wish my voice was as harsh as a crow's, then I'd have peace. (*She moves up* C.)
Alicia. Elizabeth, your lovely voice!
Richard (*rising*). We must get those letters back. (*He goes* C.)
Elizabeth. But how? I would die rather than let my father know of this.
Richard (C.). And your mother? Would she not help you if you told her?
Elizabeth. It is impossible to make her understand. I have tried. She thinks Captain Matthews admires *her*.
Alicia (*rising*). Couldn't you pretend to meet him in the garden, then Richard and I could hide behind the bushes and jump out at him when he least expected?
Elizabeth (L.C.). I never want to see or speak to him again.

RICHARD (*moving up* C.—*nobly*). You never shall, except over my dead body.

ELIZABETH (*up* L.C.—*simply*). I should indeed feel safe if you were there to protect me, Mr. Sheridan.

ALICIA (*moving up* R.C.). But what can she do?

RICHARD (*walking about*). There is only one thing to do.

ALICIA.
ELIZABETH. } Yes, yes.

RICHARD. She must elope.

ELIZABETH (*astounded*). Elope!

RICHARD. Yes. In some quiet place away from Bath you would be secure from all further insults. Moreover, you would be in a position to dictate terms to your father.

ELIZABETH. But whom can I elope with?

RICHARD. With me.

ALICIA (R.C., *triumphantly, then crossing* L.C.). I knew Dick would find a way to save you.

ELIZABETH. But I can't marry you. I hardly know you.

RICHARD (C.). I was not thinking of marriage.

ELIZABETH (L.). Mr. Sheridan! Men are all the same! And I was beginning to think you were different.

ALICIA (L.C.). But Dick isn't like a man at all. (*She moves down* L.C.) Are you, Dick?

RICHARD (C.—*stiffly*). It is because I am a man, and I hope an honourable one, that I did not intend to impose upon her helplessness. We shall travel as brother and sister.

ALICIA. Couldn't I go? (*She puts her hand out to* ELIZABETH.) Two sisters would look much more natural.

RICHARD. It is out of the question. (*Moving* L.C.) What would Father say?

ALICIA. A letter wouldn't reach him for a week, and we might be on our way home then.

RICHARD. No, Lissy.

ELIZABETH (L.C.). But I can't travel alone with you, Mr. Sheridan. Think of my reputation!

RICHARD (L.). Then we'll take a duenna.

ELIZABETH. A duenna!
ALICIA. But wouldn't that be somewhat unusual?
RICHARD. The entire circumstances are unusual. Would a duenna make you happier, Elizabeth?
ELIZABETH (*doubtfully*). You are exceedingly kind, Mr. Sheridan—but——
RICHARD (C.). I'm glad I thought of it. Now even your father will be obliged to admit that I made all our arrangements with the utmost propriety. I will leave him a note to that effect. (*He crosses up* L. *of harpsichord to* L. *of table* C.)
ELIZABETH (*moving up* L.C.). But whom can we take?
RICHARD. Shelah. She'll do anything for me.
ALICIA (*moving up* R.C.). An elopement will be very expensive, Richard. You won't be able to travel on the public coach. You'll have to take private post-chaises.
RICHARD (*airily*). I will see to all that.
ALICIA. Are you going to tell Charles?
RICHARD. No.
ALICIA (*moving down* R. *of settee*). It is fortunate Father is not at home.
RICHARD (*solemnly*). It is Fate.
ELIZABETH. Where shall we go?
RICHARD (*going to* ELIZABETH). To London first. I have some rich friends there. Then on to France. We shall be safer with the sea between Matthews and us.
ALICIA (R.C.). I can speak French, Richard, which neither of you can.
RICHARD (C.). That is an idea.
ALICIA (*eagerly*). What is?
RICHARD. Don't they take lady boarders in the convent where you were at school?
ALICIA. Yes!
RICHARD. I'll place Elizabeth there and find lodging close by for myself, until we have brought Mr. Linley to terms.
ELIZABETH (*crossing down* R.—*doubtfully*). I don't think I want to go into a convent.
RICHARD (*moving down* R.C.). It will only be for a

time, and the very sound of it is a certificate of respectability. There! Everything is settled. We shall start on the same evening that Matthews arranged to meet you. As soon as your parents are gone, you will pack what clothing you need for the journey——

ALICIA (C.). I'll help you!

ELIZABETH (*down* R.). Is it the only way, Mr. Sheridan?

RICHARD (R.C.). I think so, my dear one. (*He kisses her hand.*)

ELIZABETH (*bravely*). Then I will come with you.

(POLLY *comes in* L.)

POLLY (*down* L.). They are in bed now, Elizabeth, and I have taken away their candle.

RICHARD (*crossing* L. *to her*). Come here, Polly. We have something to tell you. Elizabeth and I are eloping the day after to-morrow. (*He brings her over to his* R. *side.*) It is a secret at present.

POLLY (*excitedly*). Oh! Can I come?

RICHARD. Not this time. I will arrange an elopement for you later.

POLLY. With you?

RICHARD. Wouldn't Charles do?

POLLY. No——

RICHARD. Charles isn't very romantic, it is true, but he is exceedingly reliable. You might do worse, Polly.

(POLLY *shakes her head.*)

ALICIA (*loyally*). Charles has an excellent disposition.

POLLY (*suddenly, crossing* R.C.). Are you running away from Captain Matthews, Elizabeth?

ELIZABETH (R.). Yes.

POLLY (R.C.—*shakily*). I hope Papa will not be angry. All the concerts will be spoilt.

ELIZABETH. I may be back before they are over—I'll come and listen.

POLLY (*breaking down*). I shall be so lonely when you're gone.

ELIZABETH. You must be brave, for my sake.

(POLLY *clings to her, sobbing.* ELIZABETH *is a little tearful herself.*)

ALICIA (*somewhat forlornly*). We'll have to console each other, Polly. I'm being left behind too.

(ELIZABETH, POLLY and ALICIA *are all crying.*)

RICHARD (L.). Now, please don't cry. It's laughing you should all be at the trick we are going to play on everyone in Bath.

(*The girls look at him silently.*)

When Matthews is safely at the other end of the garden, I will send Shelah to you with a sedan chair.

ELIZABETH (R.C.—*quickly*). Two chairs. (*She crosses* L.C.)

RICHARD. Two?

ELIZABETH. One for my luggage.

RICHARD. Two, then. I shall be waiting at the end of the Crescent and will accompany you to the London Road, where a coach will be in readiness for us. Then while Matthews cools his heels in the summer-house for an hour or two, we shall be galloping towards France as fast as our horses can carry us.

POLLY (*between sobs, moving* C.). If you're going to France, Elizabeth, you had better take your new gown, and the shoes with the silver buckles.

ALICIA (R.C., *bustling, then crossing above to* L.C.). And I must look to your clothes, Richard, and make sure that your hose is mended, and your buttons sewn fast. Since everything is settled, I think we should go home at once. There are so many things I must do. (*She crosses above to up* R.)

RICHARD (L., *unwilling to go*). Promise me that you will both go straight to your bedroom and that whoever knocks at the front door you will not open it.

ELIZABETH (*smiling*). I have all this work to do. I promised Papa it would be ready for rehearsal on Friday. I won't be able to run away with you unless it is finished.

RICHARD. Then work hard, my pet. (*Holding both of her hands.*) I will write to you to-morrow when I have completed our arrangements. Alicia will deliver the letter. It will be safer if I do not come myself.

ELIZABETH. Shall I not see you again, then?

RICHARD. Not until Shelah comes for you in the sedan chair—— Are you afraid?

ELIZABETH. A little.

(ALICIA *gives them a meaning look.*)

ALICIA (*up* R.). Well, I'm going, Dick. Come and open the front door for me, Polly.

POLLY (*as they go*). Won't Captain Matthews be furious when he finds out——

(ALICIA *and* POLLY *go out* R.)

RICHARD. You need not be afraid, Elizabeth.

ELIZABETH. Mr. Sheridan——

RICHARD. Richard! If we are to be brother and sister you must try to sound natural. Come on.

ELIZABETH (R.C., *shyly*). Dick.

RICHARD (C.). That's better.

ELIZABETH. I have not been very fortunate in my experience of the world—of gentlemen.

RICHARD (*compassionately*). We are not all unworthy, my precious.

ELIZABETH. If you call me things like that, no one will ever believe we are brother and sister.

RICHARD. But it is true. Your honour is more precious to me than my own.

ELIZABETH (*looking up at him*). This is a very serious decision for a young and ignorant girl to make alone——

RICHARD. I am young too. My youth and strength will be your shield.

ELIZABETH. I can offer no other reward than the remembrance of a grateful heart.

RICHARD. That you will remember me at all is reward enough.

ELIZABETH. I am entrusting all I possess, myself, into your hands.

RICHARD. I could never injure you. I love you too much.

Elizabeth. Others have loved me. I want to think of you as my friend.

Alicia (*outside*). Dick!

Elizabeth (*moving towards the door*). Alicia is waiting. You must go.

Richard (*coming to her*). I am your brother, your lover and your friend, Elizabeth, but I would have you think of me only as your servant. (*He falls on his knees at her feet.*) Your humble, your devoted, your faithful servant!

(Elizabeth *gazes at him in soft, grateful surprise. He bends his head before her.*)

Curtain.

ACT II

Scene 1

Scene.—*The Parlour of a convent in France. Two weeks later. It is a narrow, bare room with an uncarpeted floor. There is a window at the* L. *through which is glimpsed a green slip of garden. The door is in the centre of the back wall. On the wall at the* L. *is a large religious picture, and underneath it a small bracket holding a vase of flowers and two candlesticks. In front of it are two kneeling stools. There is a table* L.C. *with writing materials.*
(*See Ground Plan of Scene.*)

As the Curtain *rises, a small handbell is being rung gently outside.*

Richard *is alone in the room. He has been pacing up and down impatiently. He reaches the window and stands for a moment looking out. Then he begins to walk again. He is obviously very put out. The door opens and* Mère Marie Joseph *puts her head into the room inquiringly. Seeing* Richard, *her face beams with pleasure. She is very old, with a round red face, and childlike blue eyes.*

Mère Marie (*moving down* C.). Bonjour, Monsieur Sheridan. Sœur Veronique m'a dit que vous êtes arrivé. Qu'est ce qu'il vous faut à cette heure du matin ?

Richard (R.C.). I must see Elizabeth at once, Mère Marie Joseph. It is most important.

Mère Marie (C.). Mademoiselle ? Elle est dans sa chambre. La nourrice est avec elle. (*She slowly gets over the name.*) Madame O'Grah-dee, n'est ce pas ? (*She laughs delightedly at her success.*)

RICHARD (*slowly*). I have been to see Monsieur le Curé this morning.

MÈRE MARIE (*nodding*). Monsieur le Curé vient d'arriver.

RICHARD. Commend me to nuns for knowing one's thoughts!

MÈRE MARIE. Ah, que la jeunesse est belle!

RICHARD. Does that mean you approve?

(*She looks puzzled.*)

(*He goes on awkwardly.*) Voulez-vous le mariage?

MÈRE MARIE (*looking astonished for a moment*). Pardon? (*She realizes what he means.*) Ah! Je comprends! (*Primly.*) Je suis tout à fait de l'avis de Monsieur le Curé. Je conviens que dans ces circumstances, le mariage est bien souhaitable.

RICHARD (*blankly*). Bien sou—s'—— She does approve, egad!

(MÈRE MARIE *moves* L.C. *and continues to nod.* ELIZABETH *enters with* SHELAH. ELIZABETH *looks very well and happy.*)

ELIZABETH (C.). Sœur Veronique said that you wanted to see me. I was not expecting you so soon.

RICHARD (*up* R.). My business is urgent.

(ELIZABETH *is surprised.*)

MÈRE MARIE (*up* L.C.). Je dois vous quitter, mais je serai bientôt de retour—accompagnée de Monsieur le Curé. Ah, je veux que tu seras heureuse, ma mignonne!

(*She goes out laughing.*)

ELIZABETH (C.). What does she mean?

RICHARD (R., *coldly*). Something about your being happy, I believe.

ELIZABETH. How cross you look! You're not going to scold me again, are you? I thought you had said all there was to say yesterday.

RICHARD (*hotly*). Well, you did encourage them—the frogs!

ELIZABETH (*roused*). I did not.

SHELAH (*moving down* L. *of table*). Glory be to God, they're beginning again. (*She throws up her hands impatiently.*)

RICHARD (R.C.). Do you seriously ask me to believe that even a toad of a Frenchman would dare to roll his eyes at you if you had not permitted the impertinence?

ELIZABETH (*shortly*). People frequently do look at me!

RICHARD (*bitterly*). I thought you ran away with me chiefly because your modesty revolted against being publicly stared at.

ELIZABETH (*hurt*). Richard! (*She turns abruptly away to* L.C.)

SHELAH (*rushing to her defence, crossing below to* C.). And if she did smile at the gentleman, Mr. Richard, it was only because she was happy and unbeknownst to herself entirely. They meant no harm either, the poor little creatures——

RICHARD (R.C.). Poor little creatures indeed! They were grown men, older than myself.

SHELAH. They looked as scared as childer, anyway, when you went and shook your big fist at them. You're too quick-tempered the way you take people up.

RICHARD. I don't know my own sex, then? I'm nothing but a cursed fool.

SHELAH. Don't mind him, alannah! He's jealous, that's what's wrong with him.

RICHARD (*sheepishly*). It's true. I'm jealous of the very stones she walks on. (*He sees that* ELIZABETH'S *shoulders are shaking with laughter. He is tragically offended.*) You may laugh, Madam, but it is not so droll for me!

ELIZABETH (*crossing* C.). It was the way you spoke to them and the way they jabbered back. Both of you were shouting in different languages and looking as if you were going to kill each other any moment.

SHELAH (L.C., *beginning to laugh also*). Sure, the fine

anger he was in he'd have been able to best the three of them! It was a grand sight, so it was.

RICHARD (R.C.). I see nothing to laugh at. (*He crosses* L.C.)

SHELAH. Arrah, what's wrong with you? You used to like a joke as well as anyone——

RICHARD. It may please you both to know it was that jest which finally decided me to adopt the course I am about to take.

ELIZABETH. What do you mean?

RICHARD (L.C.). I have come to the conclusion that it is not suitable for you to walk outside the convent grounds. I must therefore request your promise not to do so.

(ELIZABETH *laughs*.)

ELIZABETH. Even with you to frighten the gentlemen away?

RICHARD. I have resolved to return to England immediately.

SHELAH (*amazed*). To England! (*She is* C.)

ELIZABETH (*crossing to* L.C.). And leave me here alone?

RICHARD (L.). You will not be alone. Shelah will remain. You will be perfectly safe, but I must insist that you do not venture into the streets.

ELIZABETH (L.C.). But you promised to stay with me until we heard from Papa.

RICHARD (L.). The circumstances are such that I am obliged to break that promise.

ELIZABETH (*distressed*). Have I offended you so deeply, Richard?

SHELAH (C.). More like he has come to the end of what money he managed to borrow!

RICHARD. Have you no delicacy, woman?

SHELAH (*moving* L.C.). And how can I remember to be delicate with you, Master Richard? Didn't I give you the first wash you ever had in this world? (*Crossing and sitting in the chair up* R.C.)—saving your presence for mentioning such a thing, Miss Linley.

ELIZABETH (*moving* L.—*gently*). Is that the reason, Dick?

RICHARD. I admit it is one of them. The other is my regard for your reputation.

ELIZABETH. Surely my reputation is safe, with a whole mile between your inn and my convent?

RICHARD (L.). The censorious would soon find cause for idle chatter if I remained any longer, now that my purpose has been accomplished.

ELIZABETH (L.C.). Oh, Dick, I don't want you to go!

RICHARD (*touched*). Are you not happy here?

ELIZABETH. I have been.

RICHARD (*in a low voice*). If I could stay, I would; but I dare not.

ELIZABETH (L.C.). Dare not?

RICHARD (L.). For the sake of my peace of mind. You are so close to me and so far away. I can endure it no longer.

ELIZABETH (*sadly*). I shall miss you. Will you write to me sometimes?

RICHARD (*ardently*). You know that I will.

SHELAH. When he remembers. I know that young man's promises.

ELIZABETH (*withdrawing*). Oh!

RICHARD (*crossing* C.). I shall never cease to remember—every hour—every moment. My feet will be walking about the streets of Bath, but my heart will be here, in the convent with you.

SHELAH. Then it's a fine sort of lawyer you'll be making.

ELIZABETH. When will you start?

RICHARD. The stage coach to Calais goes through to-morrow at dawn——

ELIZABETH. So soon!

RICHARD (*on her* R.—*taking her hand*). Before I go I want to ask you something.

ELIZABETH. What is it?

RICHARD. Will you marry me?

(SHELAH *rises.*)

ELIZABETH. Marry you?

RICHARD (C.). Merely in form. Believe me, I ask it only for your sake.

ELIZABETH (L.C.). Is this your honour? And I trusted you!

RICHARD. Can you not trust me a little longer? I want you to allow Monsieur le Curé to go through the form of marriage between us, solely that I may have the right to defend your virtue should it ever be called in question. I swear to you that I will hold it binding to me, only so far as you permit yourself to be bound. If you wish to marry anyone else when you return to England, you may be assured that I shall not stand in the way.

ELIZABETH (*crossing to* R. *of him*). I shall never marry.

RICHARD (L.C.). This would not be a real marriage, only the semblance of one—unless we had it confirmed in England.

SHELAH. I think it is a grand idea!

ELIZABETH. You must give me time to think.

RICHARD. In a few hours I shall be gone.

ELIZABETH. It may sound foolish to you, Richard, but even the semblance of a marriage seems a grave thing to me. Am I not alone, and in a strange country?

RICHARD (*giving in*). Very well, I shall never force you against your will. (*He crosses* L. *and picks up his hat from the table.*)

(MÈRE MARIE JOSEPH *and* MONSIEUR LE CURÉ *come in. He is carrying two books, a large one and a prayer-book which he places by the inkstand on the table. He speaks fluent but imperfect English.*)

CURÉ (*up* C.). Bonjour, mes enfants. Monsieur has given you an explication that he desire to marry himself with you, n'est ce pas? Is it also the wish of Mam'selle?

ELIZABETH (*up* L.C.). Do you think I should marry him, Father?

CURÉ. But, yes, certainement! Do you not run away together? Marriage is—convenable.

ELIZABETH (*simply*). Everyone seems to agree with you, Richard.
RICHARD (*down* L.). They know what is best for you.
ELIZABETH. I wish Papa were here to advise me—even Mama!
MÈRE MARIE (*up* R.C.). Comment, Mam'selle ne veut pas se marier?
CURÉ. Elle vacille. Elle est très jeune, la pauvre fillette.
ELIZABETH (*crossing down* L.). Richard, will you swear, on your honour, to abide by the promise you have made me?
RICHARD. I will swear it on your honour, my love, that the oath may be more binding.
ELIZABETH (L.). I will marry him, Father.
RICHARD (*kissing her hand*). Thank you.
CURÉ. Bien, it is good. (*He opens the books on the table, then taking a stole from the pocket of his soutane, puts it on very solemnly. He finds the place in his prayer-book and, holding it, waves his hand towards* SHELAH.) You, Madame O'Grady, et vous, Mère Marie Joseph, must be—how do you say?—témoins.
SHELAH (*suspiciously*). What's that? (*She moves to above* L. *of table.*)
RICHARD. I think he means you must be a witness.
SHELAH (*beaming at* M. LE CURÉ). And it's glad I'll be to see they're married good and proper!

(M. LE CURÉ *takes up a position beneath the religious picture. He motions* ELIZABETH *and* RICHARD *to the faldstools.* SHELAH *and* MÈRE MARIE JOSEPH *stand behind them.*)

CURÉ. Venez ici, s'il vous plait. The service is but short. Have you a ring, Monsieur?
RICHARD (*tapping his pocket*). I have.
ELIZABETH. Where did you get it?
RICHARD. I purchased it in Bath—before we left.
ELIZABETH (*amused in spite of herself*). You appear to have forgotten no eventuality.
CURÉ. Écoutez s'il vous plait, Mam'selle!

(SHELAH *has folded her hands and assumed a correctly solemn expression.* MÈRE MARIE JOSEPH *takes a prayer-book from the folds of her voluminous skirt and, as* M. LE CURÉ *reads the services, she murmurs some Latin responses. Their actual words are inaudible to the audience.*)

CURÉ (*breaking into English*). Richard—wilt thou take Elizabeth here present to be thy lawful wife?
RICHARD (*firmly*). I will.
CURÉ. Wilt thou, Elizabeth, take Richard here present to be thy lawful husband?
ELIZABETH (*falteringly*). I will.
CURÉ (*aside*). Prenez sa main—la main droite. Alors, repeat after me, Monsieur, I Richard, take thee Elizabeth——
RICHARD (*continuing alone*). —to be my wedded wife, to have and to hold from this day forward, for better, for worse, for richer, for poorer, in sickness and in health, till death do us part; and thereto I plight thee my troth.
CURÉ (*in a dry whisper*). You seem to know this better than I! (*Outside there is a faint noise of horses which gradually approach.*) Ego conjungo in matrimonium, in nomine Patris, et Filii, et Spiritu Sancti, Amen. (*To* RICHARD.) Put the ring on this book.

(RICHARD *does so, and the* CURÉ *blesses them.*)

Adjutorium nostrum in nomine Domini.
MÈRE MARIE. Qui fecit cœlum et terram.
CURÉ. Domine, exaudi orationem meam.
MÈRE MARIE. Et clamor meus ad te veniat.
CURÉ. Dominus vobiscum.
MÈRE MARIE. Et cum spiritu tuo.

(*The carriage has come very near. It stops.*)

CURÉ. Join hands.

(*There is a loud noise of knocking.*)

I join you in marriage.

(SHELAH *opens one eye and tries cautiously to turn her head to the window.*)

MÈRE MARIE (*softly*). C'est Monsieur le Médecin. Il fait visite à Mère Marie Therese qui est malade.

CURÉ (*to* SHELAH). The doctor to see a sick nun.

(SHELAH *composes herself anew.*)

(*To* RICHARD.) Now the ring. C'est ca ... put it on. Repeat after me. With this ring—

RICHARD (*continuing alone*). —with this ring I thee wed, with my body I thee worship, with all my worldly goods I thee endow.

SHELAH. His worldly goods!

(*There is another, louder knock, and a bell peals.*)

CURÉ. Alors, you are married. (*To* ELIZABETH.) May this be your yoke of love and peace. May you please your husband as did Rachel, be prudent as was Rebecca, long lived and faithful as Sara——

(*The bell and the knocker are sounded together very loudly and impatiently. The noise continues.*)

MÈRE MARIE (*startled*). Mon Dieu! Quel tapage! Qu'est ce qui se passe? (*She makes for the door.*)

CURÉ (*calling her back*). Un moment, ma mère. Come, mes enfants, you must all write in my book.

(*They cross to the table* L.C. *He hands the pen to* ELIZABETH.)

Mam'selle—pardon—Madame!

(*As* ELIZABETH *signs the register, the noise of bolts and chains being unfastened is heard at the outer door.*)

ELIZABETH (*rising*). Now you, Dick.

(*As* RICHARD *sits down a loud angry voice is heard outside, followed by exclamations in French.* MÈRE MARIE JOSEPH *looks astonished.*)

RICHARD (*writing*). Richard Brinsley Sheridan. There!

Curé. Mère Marie Joseph—ici.

(Mère Marie Joseph *signs rapidly, standing.*)

Mère Marie. Pardon.

(*She hurries out.*)

Richard. Now, Shelah!

(Shelah *is comically bewildered.* Richard *pushes her into the chair, puts the pen in her right hand and guides it across the page. As she rises to allow* M. le Curé *to sit, the door opens, and* Mère Marie Joseph *comes in followed by* Thomas Linley *and* Charles Sheridan. Linley *is almost beside himself with anger and exasperation.* Charles *is amused and debonair.*)

Mère Marie. Monsieur le père de Madame.

(M. le Curé *dashes off his signature, then rises to his feet, closing the book over his thumb.*)

Shelah. Glory be to God!

Elizabeth (*running eagerly to her father*). Papa!

Richard. Charles!

Linley (*responding gently, but with marked restraint*). So we have found you at last, my child.

Elizabeth (*hurt*). Aren't you glad to see me, Papa?

Linley. At least I am glad to see you looking so well.

(Elizabeth *is dismayed. She withdraws from him and looks round her in some bewilderment.*)

Richard (*to* Charles). How did you get here?

Charles (*up* L.C.). Mr. Linley brought me, at my own earnest request, because I could speak French. (*He bows to* Elizabeth, *who has turned to look at him.*) Miss Linley!

Elizabeth. Mr. Sheridan!

Richard (*bowing*). Mr. Linley, sir!—(*he indicates* M. le Curé)—M. le Curé, the convent chaplain.

Linley (c., *to* Curé). Good morning. (*To* Richard.) I want to have a talk with you, young man.

RICHARD (L.C., *politely*). Yes, sir. You received my two letters safely, I presume?

(CHARLES *moves over* R.)

LINLEY (*his anger breaking out*). Is that all you have to say to me, you damned young puppy?

ELIZABETH (R.C.). Papa!

LINLEY (C.). Be quiet, Elizabeth. (*To* SHELAH.) As for you, you old witch, I'll have you put in the ducking-stool as soon as we return to Bath.

SHELAH (R.). Mercy on us!

RICHARD (L.C.). Mr. Linley——

LINLEY. A moment, sirrah! Where is your baggage, Elizabeth? I presume you really have been staying here, and not at the public inn with that young villain.

ELIZABETH. Papa!

RICHARD (*up* L.C.). Sir, I strongly resent these aspersions on my honour——

LINLEY. Be quiet, boy! Where have you been lodging, woman?

SHELAH (*down* R., *very agitated*). I—I——

ELIZABETH (R., *proudly*). Shelah has been here, with me. She has never left my side for a moment. We have shared the same bedchamber every night since we departed from Bath.

SHELAH. It's God's truth, sir. Mr. Richard insisted upon it.

LINLEY (*more calmly*). I see. Go away, woman, and pack my daughter's baggage and your own. We shall be leaving for England at once. You may attend her on the journey.

SHELAH (*crossing up* C., *confused*). Yes, sir. (*She looks inquiringly at* RICHARD.)

LINLEY. Make haste.

SHELAH. Yes, sir.

(*She gives him a startled look and hurries out.*)

ELIZABETH. Papa, there is something I want to ask you.

LINLEY. You may tell me in the carriage.

ELIZABETH. It is a promise I want you to make.
LINLEY (*sternly*). Go and get your cloak, Elizabeth. We have no time to lose.
ELIZABETH (*wearily*). Yes, Papa.

(*She goes up* C. *and glances uncertainly at* RICHARD, *who immediately moves to the door as if to open it. As they stand there together behind* LINLEY'S *back he points to her finger. She slips off the ring and holds it in her closed hand.* RICHARD *looks at* M. LE CURÉ, *who is watching them, and puts his finger to his lips.* M. LE CURÉ *nods.* ELIZABETH *goes out.*)

LINLEY (*moving to* CHARLES *down* R., *unconscious of all this*). Charles, ask that good lady for her bill.
CHARLES (*going to* MÈRE MARIE JOSEPH). Madame, s'il vous plait——

(*They go up* R., *where* MÈRE MARIE *is seen shaking her head and arguing.*)

LINLEY (*to* M. LE CURÉ, *crossing* L.C.). You, sir, can speak English?
CURÉ (L., *gently closing his book and moving it to a tidy position on the table*). But, yes! I was once étudiant à Londres—in London. I speak English like it was my own tongue.
LINLEY. As Miss Linley's father, I would like to ask you a few questions.
CURÉ (*crossing* C.). Certainement. And is this gentleman her brother?
LINLEY. No. He is young Sheridan's brother.
CURÉ (*bringing* RICHARD *down* C.). Ah, Richard is of such a noblesse—a—a delicatesse—you understand? So different from most young men. I like him much.
LINLEY (L.C.). That, at least, is something in his favour.
CHARLES (*coming forward*). She won't take any money, sir. She says the community is in Miss Linley's debt, her music has given them such great pleasure.
CURÉ (C., *rolling his eyes to heaven*). She is a songbird.

LINLEY (*handing him a purse*). Give her something for the poor, then. I dislike to feel under an obligation.
(CHARLES *takes it and goes to* MÈRE MARIE JOSEPH. LINLEY *glances at* RICHARD.)
I would prefer that we should speak in private, sir.
CURÉ. Yes, yes! It is so fine a day. Shall we walk in the garden?
LINLEY. Thank you.
(M. LE CURÉ *opens the door and motions* LINLEY *to precede him. Before* LINLEY *can pass out,* MÈRE MARIE JOSEPH *hurries to him.*)

MÈRE MARIE (*almost weeping with gratitude*). Monsieur. Je vous remercie! Nous avons tant de pauvres. Merci! Bien merci!
LINLEY (*embarrassed*). Yes, my good woman, yes!
(MÈRE MARIE JOSEPH *hastens out.* LINLEY *looks at* M. LE CURÉ.)
CURÉ (*motioning him first*). Monsieur!
(LINLEY *goes out.*)
(*To* RICHARD, *with the air of a conspirator.*) Pas un mot! (*He goes out.* RICHARD *and* CHARLES *look at each other.*)
CHARLES (*up* R.). It appears to have been a most genteel elopement.
RICHARD (*up* R.C.). What did you expect?
CHARLES. I had hoped you would be married to her by this.
RICHARD. She is as far above me as an angel.
CHARLES (*moving* L.C.—*sighing*). True! I nearly fell in love with her myself, but I knew it to be so hopeless a pursuit, that I drew myself back in time.
RICHARD (C.). Zounds, you are a cold-blooded fish, Charles!
CHARLES (*sitting on the edge of the table*). I don't think you realize the commotion you have caused in England, Richard. Miss Linley is more famous than

any of us know. The whole country is ringing with the story of her flight. Half the papers say she has set out on a matrimonial excursion with a gentleman of title, and the other half swear she is sharing love in a cottage in some remote spot with you. I even heard in London as we came through, that I was the lucky man and that *you* were threatening to put a bullet through my heart in consequence.

RICHARD (c., *laughing*). It is to be hoped Father does not hear that version.

CHARLES (*seriously*). I have written to Father—I felt obliged to do so lest he read something in the newspapers.

RICHARD. I suppose he had to know sometime. Heaven forbid that he thinks it necessary to come home!

CHARLES. There was no time to receive his reply before we set out.

RICHARD. Where have you left Lissy?

CHARLES. She's safe enough. Mrs. Linley is looking after her.

RICHARD. Poor girl!

CHARLES (*rising*). I doubt if your trip has benefited Miss Linley as much as you intended, Richard—— (*Slyly.*) You observe that I do you the justice to think your intentions were entirely unselfish——

RICHARD. She hated singing in public; at least we can now dictate terms to her father.

CHARLES. I fear not. When he has deigned to talk to me at all on the journey, it has been to say that her contracts must be fulfilled. He let slip that she has been offered over two thousand pounds for twenty concerts! Whoever marries that girl, Dick, will command the riches of Solomon. It is a pity you didn't include a wedding in the elopement. (*He moves up* c.)

RICHARD. What a base mind you have, Charles! (*He crosses down* L.)

CHARLES. Think of the assistance you might have given your family!

RICHARD. What is Matthews doing?

CHARLES. He is spitting fire.

RICHARD. Good.
CHARLES. He has sworn to make Bath too hot to hold you.
RICHARD. I thought I had done that for him. (*He crosses up* L. *of table to* C.)
CHARLES (L.C.). There's fight in the devil yet. When he discovered your trick he became almost demented with fury. Your absence has given him ample opportunity for spreading his scandals. (*He sits on* R. *edge of table.*)
RICHARD. Scandals!
CHARLES. He has slandered you with every word he has uttered. He kept calling at our lodgings and at the Linleys' demanding us to tell him where you were. We kept assuring him we did not know, but he would not believe us. In the end we refused to open the door.
RICHARD (*delighted*). And that silenced him?
CHARLES (*rising*). No. It merely decided him to post you—I quote his own words—as a liar and a treacherous scoundrel.

(RICHARD *is taken aback. He quickly recovers.*)

RICHARD (*laughing*). Where? In some low tavern, I suppose? That won't harm me. (*He moves up* C.)
CHARLES. As a matter of fact, it was in the "Bath Chronicle."
RICHARD (*astounded*). What! In the newspapers! But——
CHARLES (*moving down* L.). I quite agree. It was a most unusual procedure. Indeed, I think he has invented a precedent. The press promises to make vastly more interesting reading in future.
RICHARD. What else did he say?
CHARLES. You may read it for yourself. Here is a cutting. (*He takes out a newspaper cutting and hands it to* RICHARD.) It amused me so highly that I purchased several copies.
RICHARD (*sitting above the table and reading*). "Mr. Richard S., having attempted, in a letter left behind him for that purpose, to account for his scandalous

method of running away from this place, by insinuations derogatory to my character; since which he neither has taken Notice of Letters——" How could I when there was not the remotest possibility of my receiving them?

CHARLES (L.C., *smiling*). Go on!

RICHARD (*reading*). "——or even informed his family of the Place where he has hid himself—I can no longer think he deserves the Treatment of a Gentleman, and therefore shall trouble myself no further about him, than, in this public Method, to post him a liar and a treacherous scoundrel." The villain! (*Rising*.) I shall challenge him for this!

CHARLES. If he hasn't challenged you first! (*He moves down* L. *of table*.)

RICHARD. I swear, here and now, that I shall not rest a night in England until I have brought him to book.

CHARLES. Don't be too rash, Dick! It will take some days to reach him.

RICHARD (*moving* C.). My head shall not rest upon a pillow until I have accomplished my purpose. I shall sit up in a chair every night between Dover and Bath.

CHARLES. You're a foolish fellow, Richard, but, zounds, if I don't admire you.

(ELIZABETH *and* SHELAH *come in dressed for the journey, followed by* MÈRE MARIE JOSEPH.)

ELIZABETH (C.). Where is Papa?

CHARLES (L.C.). In the garden talking to M. le Curé.

(ELIZABETH *is startled*.)

RICHARD (R.C.). Don't be afraid, he is only trying to find out if I have spoken the truth about our elopement.

(SHELAH *goes to the door in order to keep an eye on the passage*.)

ELIZABETH (*sadly*). I am afraid this is the end, Richard.

RICHARD. You must not say that, Elizabeth. Listen,

we may have no other opportunity for making plans. Will you arrange to see me alone when we return to Bath? We could meet at the Grotto in the Parade Gardens——

ELIZABETH (*earnestly*). Promise that somehow you will get those letters from Captain Matthews!

RICHARD. I promise.

SHELAH (*quickly*). They're coming back, Miss Linley

ELIZABETH (*holding out her hand*). Good-bye, Richard.

RICHARD (*pleading*). We can't part like this, not after all we have been through together!

CHARLES (*down* L.). Take care, Richard.

(LINLEY *and* M. LE CURÉ *come in. The latter goes above the table.*)

ELIZABETH. You see we are ready, Papa.

LINLEY. Come here, my child. (*She goes to him. He places his hand on her shoulder.*) You are very dear to me, Elizabeth, a little for your great talent, but most of all for yourself—you know that?

ELIZABETH (R.C., *in a whisper*). Yes, Papa.

LINLEY. This reverend gentleman assures me that Mr. Sheridan has behaved as honourably towards you as even your father could wish. Is that true?

ELIZABETH (*proudly*). Yes, Papa.

LINLEY (*grandly, crossing* R.). Then I will shake your hand, Mr. Sheridan. We are friends.

RICHARD (*down* R.). And may I travel back with you, sir?

(M. LE CURÉ *has quietly returned to the table, where he begins writing on a slip of paper.*)

LINLEY. As to that——

ELIZABETH. Please, Papa.

LINLEY. You may. But when we reach Bath, our ways shall part. Henceforth you and my daughter shall meet only as acquaintances. You understand that.

RICHARD. But, sir——!

LINLEY (R.C., *sternly*). It is my wish, and I mean to

see it is obeyed. Charles, go and tell the coachman that we shall all dine at the inn before we proceed.

CHARLES (*crossing* C.). Yes, sir.

(CHARLES *goes out.*)

LINLEY (*up* C.). Make your farewells, Elizabeth; and please be brief.

(*He goes out.*)

RICHARD. I'll think of some plan. Lissy will bring you a message—— Promise that you will see me.

ELIZABETH (*evading him*). Please, Richard—— (*She goes to* MÈRE MARIE JOSEPH.) Good-bye, Mère Marie.

MÈRE MARIE (*kissing her on both cheeks*). Au revoir, ma chérie, au revoir.

ELIZABETH. Good-bye, Monsieur. (*She turns to go.*)

CURÉ (*coming to her with his slip of paper*). Madame —you forget your lines of marriage!

(ELIZABETH *takes it, and then suddenly, to everyone's surprise, she bursts into tears.*)

ELIZABETH (*sobbing*). I don't want to go back. I don't want to go back.

(*She runs out blindly.* RICHARD *immediately follows her.*)

CURTAIN.

SCENE 2

SCENE.—*An upper room at the White Hart Inn, Bath, about midnight, four days later.*

It is a large bare room, which acts as a sort of informal mess for certain officers who are spending the season at Bath and putting up at the Inn. The firegrate is on the right side, and above it is a door leading to CAPTAIN MATTHEWS' *bedroom. In the centre of the back wall is the door to the corridor. The window is at the* L. *There is a table in the centre of the room, littered*

with belts, spurs, swords and pistols. A dresser placed against the back wall holds pewter mugs and plates, decanters and glasses. Below the window is a writing-table with paper, pens and ink. There is an armchair beside the fire, and several other straight-backed chairs are placed about the room.
(*See Ground Plan of Scene.*)

When the CURTAIN *rises,* CAPTAIN KNIGHT *is sitting* L. *of the table oiling and polishing his pistols. He has removed his sword belt, his coat is unbuttoned, and he wears slippers. He lays down his rag and peers into the lock of a pistol with evident satisfaction, then takes up another and begins polishing again, humming a little song.* MATTHEWS *comes in. He is tired and cross. He throws his hat on the dresser up* R.C.

MATTHEWS (*up* C., *impatiently*). That fool of a landlord kept me waiting five minutes at the door before he let me in.

KNIGHT (*merely amused*). He is getting deafer every day.

MATTHEWS. Why he should want to bolt and bar the door before all his guests are in, I cannot conceive. He must have been aware that I was still out. (*He throws* KNIGHT *his coat.*)

KNIGHT (*rising and going* R.). Yes, he knew, but you are so much later than I anticipated that I came to the conclusion that you did not intend returning to-night, and I told him he might lock up. (*He puts the coat below the fire.*)

MATTHEWS (*sourly*). You had better not come to conclusions in the future. So much thinking is bad for you. (*He begins taking off his gloves.*)

KNIGHT (R.). If I were not your kinsman, Tom, I would long ago have resented your manners sufficiently to ask for satisfaction. It wasn't my fault that Miss Linley ran away with young Sheridan. As a matter of fact, I rather fancied her myself.

MATTHEWS (*savagely*). Be silent!

KNIGHT. *And* I think I should have had more chance

than you. I'm nearer her own age, and without the least vanity; I think I may say, I am decidedly better favoured.

MATTHEWS (*crossing L.—furiously*). You may forget our kinship, you young insolent dog! We'll fight to-morrow morning. You had better spend the night writing farewell letters to your mother.

KNIGHT (*calmly*). Don't be a fool, Tom.

(MATTHEWS *glares at him and makes as if to speak, then thinks the better of it.*)

MATTHEWS (*crossing up* C.). I ordered some brandy. That fellow must be distilling it!

(*He strides to the door and opens it with a flourish. The* LANDLORD *is outside with a tray, which, in his fright, he nearly drops. He is a shuffling old fellow and very deaf, and he speaks in a thin quavering voice.*)

LANDLORD. Lud, sir, you gave me quite a turn! (*He shuffles into the room and puts down the tray on the table.*) Did you want something, sir?

MATTHEWS. No. Get out!

LANDLORD (*politely*). Pardon?

MATTHEWS (*shouting*). Get out!

LANDLORD. Certainly, sir, certainly.

(*He goes out.* MATTHEWS *pours out a glassful for himself, and drinks it off at a gulp.* KNIGHT *watches him with interest.* MATTHEWS *pours out another glassful.*)

KNIGHT (*admiringly*). How splendidly you do drink, Tom! And I'll wager that is by no means your first couple of glasses this evening.

MATTHEWS. Hold your tongue.

(*Still holding the glass, he throws himself in the armchair by the fire, and sprawls with his feet apart.*)

KNIGHT. Love never takes me that way. I always feel holy and uplifted; and I want to write verse.

MATTHEWS. Damned fool!

(*There is a loud knocking downstairs.*)

KNIGHT. Someone else appears to be locked out. I thought all the other fellows were in.

(*The noise becomes tremendous. He gets up and, going to the window, peers through the panes.*)

It's so plaguey dark out there.

(*The knocking goes on.*)

Zounds, what a hurry the man is in!

(*The* LANDLORD *comes in with a lantern.*)

LANDLORD. Did anyone knock, sir?

(MATTHEWS *glances at him and mutters impatiently to himself.*)

KNIGHT. I fancy there is someone tapping at the front door.

LANDLORD (*uncertainly*). It is very late. These night-travellers bode no good. If it is another runaway couple, I must positively refuse to receive them. I have no wish to be threatened by any more angry fathers——

(*Another knock.*)

Excuse me, sir.

(*He goes to the window and, opening the casement, holds out his lantern to see who is there.*)

KNIGHT. Merely two gentlemen this time, Landlord!

LANDLORD (*calling*). What do you want? My inn is full up.

RICHARD (*outside*). Is Captain Matthews in?

KNIGHT (*excitedly*). Sheridan, by all that's wonderful! Tom, did you hear that?

(MATTHEWS *has risen to his feet.*)

MATTHEWS. What does he want?

LANDLORD. I can't hear what he is saying. (*He raises his voice.*) It is too late. I am going to bed.

RICHARD. I don't care. Tell Captain Matthews I must see him.

MATTHEWS. Must!

(*The* LANDLORD *looks inquiringly at* KNIGHT.)

KNIGHT (*shutting the casement and shouting*). He is asking for Captain Matthews.

LANDLORD (*nodding*). Yes, sir. (*He turns as if to make for the door.*) I'll let him in.

MATTHEWS (R.). Stop! I won't see him. (*Shouting.*) He can call to-morrow.

LANDLORD. Yes, sir. (*He opens the window and calls.*) He can't see you to-night, sir. He has gone to bed.

RICHARD. Get him up. I want to speak to him.

(*The* LANDLORD *looks at* KNIGHT *questioningly.*)

CHARLES (*outside*). You'll have the whole neighbourhood up, Dick. We'd better wait.

RICHARD. I won't. Open this door.

(*He begins to kick it wildly. Even the* LANDLORD *hears him.*)

LANDLORD. Oh, sir! You'll bring the watch.

RICHARD. If you don't let me in, I will break down the door.

KNIGHT (*putting his head out*). Not that door, dear Sheridan. It has withstood two centuries of battering.

RICHARD. So you're there, Knight. Let me in!

KNIGHT (*closing the window*). Go home to bed.

(*The noise begins again and distant shouts are heard.*)

LANDLORD (*up* R.C., *to* MATTHEWS). Hadn't you better speak to him, sir? The whole town will know he is at the door, and my inn has always been respectable.

MATTHEWS. Very well. (*He takes the* LANDLORD'S *lantern and, crossing* L., *holds it out of the window so that it lights up his face.*) What do you want?

RICHARD. I want to speak to you. Open the door!

MATTHEWS. The key has been lost. You will have to wait until morning.

RICHARD. Then I'll knock until daylight. (*He begins again.*)

MATTHEWS (*banging the window shut*). Oh, let him in!

(*He signals to the* LANDLORD, *who goes out.* MATTHEWS *paces up and down.*)

(*Crossing* R.C.) What the devil can he want?

KNIGHT. To run you through, probably. I am glad I was still up.

MATTHEWS. You're an irresponsible fool, Ned.

KNIGHT (L., *lightly*). He's out for bloody sword and gun fighting, I'll be sworn. (*Moving* L.C.) What will you wager?

LANDLORD (*outside*). This way, sirs.

(*He ushers* RICHARD *and* CHARLES *into the room, then stands waiting.*)

RICHARD (*crossing* R.C.). You may go, Landlord.

LANDLORD (*up* C.). What?

KNIGHT (*shouting and gesticulating*). Go—to bed.

LANDLORD. But who will let them out?

RICHARD (*shouting in his ear*). Whichever of us is alive!

LANDLORD. God-a-mercy!

KNIGHT. Don't mind him. Go away!

(*He pushes the* LANDLORD *out.* CHARLES *closes the door.*)

MATTHEWS. What do you mean by this conduct, sir?

RICHARD. Precisely what I have just indicated. During my absence you dared to publish certain slanders concerning me in the Bath papers. Doubts of my honour are doubts of hers! I have sworn never to rest until I have challenged you. It is now four nights since I went to bed. I refuse to sit up a fifth.

MATTHEWS. Do not, I beg, deprive yourself of so much sleep on my account. If it is a fight you want, we can discuss it in the morning. (*Crossing down* L. *for candle.*) I am tired, and you must be thoroughly fatigued after so long and, may I say, so wakeful a journey.

RICHARD. The journey was not in the least fatiguing. I travelled in pleasant company.

MATTHEWS. Your brother's, I presume.

RICHARD. In Mr. Linley's, Miss Linley's and in my just anger's.

MATTHEWS. What! (*To* CHARLES.) Is this true? (*He moves up* L.C.) Has Miss Linley returned?

CHARLES (*at door* C.). She has.

MATTHEWS. Then I will call on her father to-morrow, immediately I have breakfasted.

CHARLES (*calmly*). I doubt if you will be received.

MATTHEWS. And pray why not? Because your brother has told him some lies?

CHARLES. No, because Miss Linley has told him the truth.

MATTHEWS (*taken aback*). Miss Linley!

CHARLES. In fact, it would be as well if you retired from Bath discreetly before her story becomes common property.

RICHARD (*up* R.C.). Not before he has fulfilled his obligation to me!

MATTHEWS (*sneering*). There is no question of my retiring from Bath. You don't happen to know, apparently, that I also can make the terms of certain letters she wrote me common property.

RICHARD (*rushing at him*). You deserve to die for that!

CHARLES (*restraining him*). You promised to keep calm, Dick!

MATTHEWS. Mr. Linley is the person to decide whether my behaviour to his daughter has been dishonourable or not. I fail to see that I am answerable to a pair of hot-headed schoolboys.

CHARLES (*quietly*). You will at least remember to-morrow that we warned you of the reception you are likely to meet.

MATTHEWS. I have said all I mean to say on the subject. If I hear anything further of this slander against my character, I will consult an attorney and publish a further statement. Captain Knight will see you out—good night! (*He makes for his bedroom door up* R.)

RICHARD (*placing himself before the door*). Wait a moment!

KNIGHT (*superciliously*). Come, Mr. Sheridan, it is too late an hour for these stage heroics——

CHARLES (*very quietly, moving down* L.C.). Do I understand that your reference to my father's profession is intended as an insult?

KNIGHT (L., *loftily*). Certainly, if you please to recognize it as such.

CHARLES (*still more quietly*). Then may I return it with interest? (*He flicks* KNIGHT'S *face with his glove.*) My second will wait upon you to-morrow morning. (*He moves down* L.)

KNIGHT (*amazed*). Did you hear that, Tom? He dares to challenge *me*! (*He crosses* C.)

RICHARD. Good for you, Charles!

MATTHEWS. One is not obliged to accept a challenge except from one's social equals.

RICHARD (*taking a step towards him*). What did you say?

(CHARLES *merely smiles.*)

MATTHEWS (*to* RICHARD). Let me pass, fellow.

RICHARD. Not until I am ready, fellow.

MATTHEWS. Must I kick you out of my way?

RICHARD (*coming a step nearer*). You have my permission to try, sir!

(MATTHEWS *involuntarily backs before him.*)

MATTHEWS (*after a perceptible pause*). What precisely is the object of this unmannerly obstruction?

RICHARD. I have already told you.

MATTHEWS. You surely do not expect that I can seriously accept a challenge from *you*?

RICHARD. I not only expect, I intend that you shall fight.

MATTHEWS. And when, pray?

RICHARD. Here and now. Your cousin can act as your second, Charles will be mine.

KNIGHT (*crossing down* R. *to the fire*). Preposterous!

MATTHEWS (*trying to laugh*). Absurd!

RICHARD. Why not?

MATTHEWS. At this hour?

RICHARD. I thought it would be obvious even to your mean intelligence that I am unwilling to spend another night out of bed.

KNIGHT. Whoever heard of such an insane proposal?

MATTHEWS (*moving* C.). I refuse to consider it.

RICHARD (*lightly*). I am beginning to understand, Charles. They don't want to fight.

MATTHEWS. You're an insolent puppy, sir!

RICHARD (*up* R.C., *hotly*). And you're a coward, sir!

MATTHEWS. What!

RICHARD. I repeat it—a coward! You are afraid to accept my challenge. I must force you. (*He gives him a blow on the cheek.*) Now will you fight?

MATTHEWS (*quietly*). So you want to die, young fellow?

RICHARD. No. Nor do I wish to take your life. I am somewhat anxious that you should live to savour your humiliation to the full. I shall fight only to win your sword.

MATTHEWS (*bowing ironically*). At your service.

KNIGHT (*crossing up* R., *urgently*). Are you aware that he is considered the finest swordsman in the regiment?

RICHARD (*airily*). And the best whist player, I understand.

MATTHEWS (*impatiently*). Fool!

KNIGHT. But he will kill you!

RICHARD. You think the encounter is too uneven? Your second seems to prefer some other means of fighting, Captain Matthews. Shall we say pistols instead?

KNIGHT. Pistols!

RICHARD. Then I should not be at such disadvan-

tage. I see there are some here already primed——
(*He walks towards the table and to* L. *of it.*)

MATTHEWS. Are you seriously suggesting we duel with pistols—here?

RICHARD (*fingering one*). Why not?

KNIGHT. The room isn't wide enough.

RICHARD (*taking up the gun*). The width of the table is sufficient. We could stand on either side and take aim—— (*He takes aim at* MATTHEWS.) So. (*Casually.*) Is this gun loaded?

KNIGHT (*shrieking*). Put it down!

MATTHEWS. This is no time for jesting.

RICHARD (*putting down the pistol*). I am in deadly earnest.

KNIGHT. He will have to take his chance with swords, Tom.

CHARLES (L., *dryly*). Besides, swords are the proper weapons for *gentlemen*.

MATTHEWS (R.C., *drawing his sword*). You will bear witness to-morrow, Mr. Charles Sheridan, that I had no wish to kill your brother.

RICHARD (L.C., *drawing his sword*). You will bear witness to-morrow, Captain Edward Knight, that even the finest swordsman in the regiment was no match for the favourite pupil of Henry Angelo.

MATTHEWS (*dropping the point of his sword*). } What!
KNIGHT.

MATTHEWS (*after a moment, flatly*). It is a lie.

CHARLES (L.). Oh, no. Richard is positively his best pupil, though (*he glances ironically at* KNIGHT) I am not considered much inferior myself.

MATTHEWS (R.C.). I refuse to fight.

RICHARD (L.C.). You hear that, Captain Knight? He withdraws at the very mention of my master's name. You will bear witness to that, also.

MATTHEWS. The whole business is fantastic. That is why I withdraw.

RICHARD (*taking some sheets of paper from his pocket*). May I ask you for some ink?—Ah, I see there are writing materials all ready laid out for us. (*He brings ink and pens from the bureau to the table.*) Will you sit here, Captain Matthews?

MATTHEWS (*crossing* L.C.). What child's-play is this?

RICHARD. You will write at my dictation a complete retraction of your accusation against my honour——

MATTHEWS (*bluffing*). What accusation?

RICHARD (*down* L.). The retraction to be published in the "Bath Chronicle." (*He holds out a pen.*)

MATTHEWS. I refuse.

RICHARD. Very well then, you must fight.

KNIGHT. Fight, Tom! Even if he is a fine swordsman, he can't be as good as you. You must now, for your reputation's sake.

RICHARD. Mark that, Charles! Safety first and honour afterwards.

MATTHEWS (R.C.). Blast you for an insolent scullion! I will fight! (*He takes off his coat.*)

(KNIGHT *moves brandy from table to dresser.*)

RICHARD (*taking off his coat*). Excellent!

KNIGHT. Are you ready?

CHARLES. Yes!

KNIGHT (*loudly*). Go to your guard!

(*They face each other.*)

MATTHEWS (*shouting as he raises his blade*). Hold up the candles, Ned! I fight to kill!

RICHARD (*exultantly*). Agreed!

(KNIGHT *holds up candles.* CHARLES *watches the sword-play intently, moving as the combatants move.* MATTHEWS *and* RICHARD *begin to fight, cautiously at first, then more recklessly.* MATTHEWS *gradually forces* RICHARD *back towards the window, and, in the course of his advantage, pricks* RICHARD *in the arm.* RICHARD *winces and starts back momentarily, but almost immediately recovers and, setting his lips, fights with greater determination.* MATTHEWS *is pushed back to the other end of the room. They are both becoming exhausted and panting in great gasps. Suddenly* RICHARD *sees an advantage and, with a low cry, thrusts and turns*

MATTHEWS' *sword out of line, then, with a swift movement, he seizes* MATTHEWS' *right wrist in his left hand, and holding* MATTHEWS' *sword high over his head, points his own at* MATTHEWS' *breast.*)

KNIGHT (*dashing forward*). Don't kill him! (*Panic-stricken, he seizes hold of* RICHARD'S *arm.*)

RICHARD (*shouting*). His life is mine!

KNIGHT. Beg your life, Tom! Quick, or you're a dead man!

RICHARD. Let go, damn you. Let go!

KNIGHT. Tom!

MATTHEWS (*collapsing*). I beg my life—I beg my life.

(RICHARD *lets go unwillingly.* MATTHEWS' *sword arm falls.*)

KNIGHT. There, he has begged his life, now that's the end of it. (*He puts the sword away.*)

CHARLES (R., *impatiently*). Your conduct is most irregular, Captain Knight. When Captain Matthews' sword was in my brother's power and he attempted no further injury, you should not have interfered.

KNIGHT (C., *hotly*). I did it to prevent mischief.

MATTHEWS (L., *meaningly*). Mr. Sheridan was very obliged to you for your interposition.

RICHARD (L.C., *furiously*). Are you daring to imply that your second's action was on *my* account, and not on *yours*?

KNIGHT (*hastily*). No, Tom. Before I interposed both swords were in Mr. Sheridan's power.

MATTHEWS (*deliberately*). I never quitted my sword

RICHARD (*wildly*). Then you will quit now, sir, or go to your guard again!

(MATTHEWS *hesitates. He gives* RICHARD *a black look.*)

KNIGHT. You mustn't fight again, Tom. He'll kill you.

CHARLES. So, after all, you are obliged to admit that he is a credit to his fencing master!

KNIGHT (*urgently*). Tom!
MATTHEWS. Very well. I give in.

(*He throws his sword on the floor between himself and* RICHARD. RICHARD *puts his own back into the scabbard.*)

RICHARD. Thank you. (*He goes to pick up* MATTHEWS' *sword, but in bending, suddenly hesitates and puts his hand to his chest.*) Pick it up for me, Charles.

(CHARLES *does so.*)

CHARLES (*as he hands it to* RICHARD). Is anything wrong?

RICHARD (L.C.). It's nothing. (*He smiles.*) I am breathless, that's all. (*He turns to* MATTHEWS.) Now, sir, the letters first.

(MATTHEWS *takes a small bundle from his pocket and tosses it on the table.*)

RICHARD. I am greatly obliged. (*He puts them in his own pocket.*) Won't you sit down? There is still that little paragraph for the "Bath Chronicle."

MATTHEWS (R., *sulkily*). I will not write it.

RICHARD. Yes, you shall! Unless you prefer that a full account of to-night's duel is published instead. Either suits me.

CHARLES. In fact, the latter would be the better for us. (*He brings candle to table.*)

MATTHEWS (*crossing* C.—*ungraciously*). Very well. I'll do it. (*He sits down.*)

RICHARD (L.C., *dictating*). "Being convinced that the expressions I have used to Mr. Sheridan's disadvantage were the effects of Passion and Misrepresentation, I retract what I have said and beg his pardon for my advertisement in the 'Bath Chronicle.'" That is all—— Thank you.

(MATTHEWS *throws down his pen.*)

Sign it!

(MATTHEWS *signs, then rises, pushing the chair back.*)

I swear, on my honour, that what has passed between us will never be mentioned by me, unless you force me to it. Here is your sword. (*He gives it to* MATTHEWS *and bows.*) Good night.

(MATTHEWS *puts his sword back into the scabbard.*)

MATTHEWS (*sulkily*). Good night.

(*He goes out into the bedroom banging the door.* RICHARD *leans on the back of a chair as if for support and clutches at his heart again.*)

CHARLES (*taking up* MATTHEWS' *note*). Perhaps you will be kind enough to see us out?

(KNIGHT *goes out without a word.* RICHARD *begins pulling at his shirt collar.*)

(*Looking at the paper and laughing.*) Now we'll go home to bed.

(RICHARD *does not reply.* CHARLES *looks up at him.*)

(*Sharply.*) Why, what is the matter?

RICHARD (*strangely*). I think I'm hurt. (*He pitches forward to the floor.*)

CHARLES (*kneeling beside him, distractedly*). Dick! Dick! (*He tears open his waistcoat. The shirt beneath is stained with blood.*)

(KNIGHT *comes back with a lantern.*)

KNIGHT (*insolently*). Are you ready?
CHARLES (*horrified*). God! Through his heart!

CURTAIN.

ACT III

SCENE 1

SCENE.—*A room at the* SHERIDANS' *house, next evening. It is a pleasant, shabby room, comfortable but quite undistinguished except for the number of books with which it is littered. The fireplace is on the left, and in front of it is a settee. There are two doors, one opening into the wall down* R. *from the passage outside, and the other above the fireplace, leading to* MR. SHERIDAN'S *study. The other furniture consists of bookcases, several chairs, a small table and a harpsichord. The latter is draped with a cloth and has so many objects heaped upon it that one knows at a glance that it is seldom used. On the mantelpiece is an enormous pile of letters. Outside, the evening sky is still bright.*
(*See Ground Plan of Scene.*)

When the CURTAIN *rises,* ALICIA *is standing at the window, peering anxiously through the panes. Almost immediately* SHELAH *comes in, wearing her bonnet and cloak. She looks grave and important.* ALICIA *immediately rushes to her side.*

ALICIA (*urgently*). Have you found them?
SHELAH (*briefly, moving* C.). I have not.
ALICIA. But you've heard something?
SHELAH. I have. (*She begins taking off her bonnet.*)
ALICIA. What is it? Did they really go to challenge that horrid Captain Matthews? Oh, why don't you answer me, Shelah! Are they safe?
SHELAH. Ay, by all accounts—at least Mr. Charles is.
ALICIA. And Dick—what about Dick?
SHELAH. What about him, indeed—(*crossing up* L.C.

and putting her bonnet on the table) the young divil, for divil he is—(*she recollects herself and looks piously to heaven*) if he isn't an angel by this.

ALICIA (*terror-stricken*). Shelah! My darling Dick, he isn't—he isn't dead?

SHELAH (*up* L.C.). I'm certain sure he isn't. It's my opinion it would take more than Captain Matthews to let the soul loose out of that gossoon. But half the people in Bath seem to think he's dead and gone this moment.

ALICIA (*up* C.). Doesn't anyone know for sure?

SHELAH. Ah, they think they do, but they do not.

ALICIA. What are they saying?

SHELAH (*impatiently*). Amn't I trying to tell you as fast as I can? Half the town say that Master Richard fought Captain Matthews last night with swords, and the other half say it was pistols; and a whole lot more say it was Mr. Richard that was kilt, and the rest say it was the Captain; and some say they were only wounded.

ALICIA. Wounded!

SHELAH. Well, some say it was a pistol shot through his right eye, and more say it was his left leg that's broken.

ALICIA. But who?

SHELAH. How the divil can I tell, when everybody says it was someone different?

ALICIA. Then where did they fight?

SHELAH (*going to the fire*). That's another thing nobody seems to agree about. Half of them told me——

ALICIA (*almost shouting*). Where are they *now*?

SHELAH. Some say——

ALICIA (*sobbing*). You're a cruel, stupid old woman, Shelah. I wish I had never trusted you to go—— (*She makes for the door* R.)

SHELAH. Where are you going?

ALICIA (*loudly*). Out! To discover the truth!

(*She flings the door open in the face of* THOMAS SHERIDAN, *who is coming in.*)

(*Recoiling.*) Father! (*She breaks to* R.C.)

SHELAH. Glory be God—it's himself!

SHERIDAN. Where are you going in such haste, Alicia?

ALICIA (R.C.). Nowhere, Father.

SHERIDAN (*down* R.). Did I not hear you say, or rather shout, in a manner quite unbecoming to my daughter, that you were about to discover Truth?— Truth, the knowledge of which has evaded the searchings of philosophers and scholars from the beginning of time?

ALICIA. Oh, Father! Richard has been killed!

SHERIDAN (*sternly*). What nonsense is this?

ALICIA. He went out last night with Charles, and they haven't come back yet. Shelah and I *knew* they were going to challenge Captain Matthews——

SHERIDAN. A moment, Alicia! Do I understand that *Charles* is associated with Richard in some excursion?

ALICIA. Yes. Charles didn't tell us that they were going out to fight Captain Matthews, but we *knew*. Oh, Father——

SHERIDAN. If Charles is with Richard, I do not see what cause you have for anxiety. (*Crossing below to* C.) Charles is a most sensible young man. He takes after me in that respect. I can't think where Richard's recklessness and irresponsibility comes from. It must be somewhere on your poor dear mother's side——

ALICIA. But, Father, we don't know where they are now; and everybody says Richard has been fighting duels.

SHERIDAN (*going to the fire*). Richard is not old enough to fight duels.

ALICIA. He is twenty-one——

SHERIDAN. Only a fool could take him seriously. This Captain Matthews on the one occasion of our meeting did not give me the impression of being a fool—far from it.

ALICIA (*despairing, moving* C.). You don't understand! (*She goes up* L.C.)

SHERIDAN (*moving up* L.C. *to her—becoming roused*). I understand that both you and your brother have behaved in so undutiful a fashion that your father has been obliged to beg leave of absence and travel night and day from Dublin.

(SHELAH *has been sidling towards the door. He rounds on her.*)

As for you, you—antiquated Eve—I shall have something to say to *you* later.

SHELAH. Yes, sir.

(*She edges out* R.)

SHERIDAN (*taking up a commanding attitude on the hearthrug*). Sit down, Alicia.

(*She does so in the armchair* C.)

I wish to question you.

ALICIA. Yes, Father.

SHERIDAN. I am still incompletely acquainted with the events which have occurred since your brother Charles first wrote to inform me of Richard's preposterous elopement with Shelah——

ALICIA (*quickly*). It was with Betsy——

SHERIDAN (*impatiently*). I am aware that Miss Linley was the principal instigator. Your brother mentioned that the girl's father was about to follow her to France. Did he do so?

ALICIA. Yes, and Charles went too—(*swiftly*) because he could speak French.

SHERIDAN (*thundering—stepping to her*). And where did *you* stay?

ALICIA. With Mrs. Linley.

SHERIDAN. I dislike that woman. I am deeply chagrined that you should have laid me under an obligation to her.

ALICIA. There was nowhere else for me to go. (*She rises, but, quelled by his look, sits again.*)

SHERIDAN. The blame lies with Richard. When did the young villain return?

ALICIA. Last night. While he was away, Captain Matthews posted him in the "Bath Chronicle" and so, when Richard found out, he had to challenge him. (*She begins to cry.*) I think he must have taken Charles with him to be his second.

SHERIDAN (L.). Do you imply that on his return he went straight out to find Matthews?

ALICIA. He had a good wash first, of course, and something to eat.

SHERIDAN. And something to drink too, I'll warrant! What time was this?

ALICIA. About midnight.

SHERIDAN. Eighteen hours ago. Then where are they?

ALICIA. We don't know. (*Crying.*) One half of Bath says he is wounded, and the other half says he is dead. (*Her sobs choke her.*)

SHERIDAN. Quit making that noise!

(*He paces up and down, frowning. There is a knock outside.* ALICIA *lifts her head. It comes again.* SHERIDAN *halts abruptly.* ALICIA *flies to the window and tries to look down into the street below.* SHERIDAN *decides to return to the hearthrug. He takes up a negligent attitude, with one elbow on the mantelpiece. He sees the heap of letters, unopened. Forgetting his pose, he draws them towards him and peers through his eyeglass. Apparently they are addressed to him. With an air of surprise he tears one open and begins to read.*)

ALICIA (*running to the door*). I heard the front door close.

SHERIDAN (*shouting*). Come back at once and sit down!

(ALICIA *returns and sits down again, watching the door.* SHERIDAN *tears open another letter, and another. He utters an exclamation of helpless fury. He begins opening the whole collection. The door opens and* SHELAH *ushers in* LINLEY.)

SHELAH (*hastily*). Mr. Linley to see Miss Lissy.

(*She shuts the door on herself quickly. The two men stare at each other.* ALICIA *rises and goes up* R.C.)

LINLEY (C.). I was not aware you had returned to Bath, Mr. Sheridan.
SHERIDAN. I arrived but an hour since. (*Balefully.*) And I might observe, Mr. Linley, that my return has obliged me to relinquish a most lucrative engagement in Dublin.
LINLEY (*stiffly*). Your anxiety was natural.
SHERIDAN (*angrily, stepping* L.C.). Anxiety, sir! Anxiety! I doubt if you have any conception of my feelings when I learnt what had transpired during my absence——
LINLEY (*rousing*). You appear to forget that your son carried off my daughter——
SHERIDAN (*shouting*). I forget nothing, sir! Let me tell you that my son is far too young and foolish to plan so elaborate an elopement. It was your daughter, sir, that led him astray——
LINLEY (*shouting also*). My daughter! You dare to insinuate that my daughter—— Damme, sir, you're a bigger rogue than your son!
SHERIDAN (*striding to the door* R. *and flinging it open*). Leave my house, sir!
ALICIA (*stepping down* R.C., *pleading*). But we don't even know why he came, Father. Mr. Linley, have you heard any news of Richard?
LINLEY. I have heard a thousand rumours, but no facts.
ALICIA (*crossing* L., *wailing*). I know he's dead! (*She sits below the fireplace.*)
SHERIDAN (*down* R.). Kindly control yourself, Alicia. Your lack of restraint before this—gentleman, is most mortifying. Will you go, sir?
LINLEY. Most certainly I shall go. But I insist that you shall hear me first.
SHERIDAN. Insist?
LINLEY (C., *ignoring him*). I thought it best to send my daughter to Clifton Wells with her sister Polly. I intend them to remain there until scandal-mongers have found some other matter to wag their tongues over. I came to say, Miss Sheridan—and the reception I have

been accorded has considerably strengthened my resolve—that I have decided my family shall hold no further communication with yours.

ALICIA. What about my music lessons?

LINLEY. They are at an end. I have forbidden your brother to correspond in any way with my daughters. I must now request a promise that you, also, will obey my injunction.

SHERIDAN (*grandly*). You may rest completely assured, sir, that in the future *my* family will not honour yours with our acquaintance.

(*While they have been speaking, the sound of a horse and carriage has approached. Now it stops outside.* ALICIA *turns and runs to the window. The men disregard her.*)

LINLEY. I imagined the honour was yours, sir. (*He bows stiffly.*) Good day.

SHERIDAN (*bowing and opening the door* R.). Good day.

ALICIA (*with a cry of joy*). Richard! Richard!

(*She runs out past her father.*)

SHERIDAN. What was that?

LINLEY. Did she say, Richard?

(*They look at each other in surprise.* ALICIA *appears in the doorway.*)

ALICIA (*excitedly*). He's alive, Father. He's alive! (*She disappears again.*)

SHERIDAN. I had no doubt that he was alive. It would take a downpour of fire and brimstone from heaven to destroy that young villain.

LINLEY. Not a villain, Mr. Sheridan. A rogue, perhaps, but not a villain.

SHERIDAN. Permit me to call my own son what I choose, Mr. Linley!

(ALICIA *backs into the room before* CHARLES, RICHARD *and* SHELAH, *who are entering.* RICHARD *has his left arm in a sling and his left sleeve pinned to his coat.*

He is pale but walks with a firm step. When he sees his father he hesitates, then sways unsteadily on his feet. He is immediately supported on one side by CHARLES *and on the other side by* SHELAH. *Recovering himself with an effort, he achieves a brave, feeble smile.*)

RICHARD. Father!
CHARLES. We did not expect you home so soon.
SHERIDAN. That is abundantly obvious.
RICHARD (*closing his eyes*). I think I am going to faint.

(*He is led to the armchair* C., *where* ALICIA *fusses over him solicitously.*)

SHERIDAN. That is right! Take refuge in histrionics.
LINLEY (R., *to the air*). He has undoubtedly inherited all the family talent.
SHERIDAN (*loudly*). Shelah!

(*She starts guiltily.*)

Shut that door!

(*She makes to go out.*)

No. I wish you to remain here.

(*She looks exceedingly uncomfortable.*)

Take a seat, Mr. Linley.

(SHELAH *brings a chair from* R. *to down* R.C.)

LINLEY. You will recollect, sir, I was on the point of leaving your house.
SHERIDAN. I will be obliged for your company a moment longer.

(LINLEY *sits.*)

Stop fussing over your brother, Alicia, and sit down.

(ALICIA *obeys meekly, sitting at* R. *end of settee.*)

I have something to say that concerns you all. (*He strides to the mantelpiece, and, seizing the letters, takes up his old position on the hearthrug.*) Now, Charles, will you kindly begin by explaining where you and your brother have been since you left this house last evening?

CHARLES. At the White Hart Inn, sir.

SHERIDAN. The White Hart! (*He points a shaking finger at* RICHARD.) So, he's been hurt in a drunken brawl! I might have known it.

CHARLES. Not at all, sir. He was wounded in an honourable encounter with Captain Matthews, in which I acted as his second. I am happy to say we were completely victorious.

ALICIA. I should have known Heaven would defend the right!

SHERIDAN. When and where did this duel take place?

CHARLES. At the inn, about half-past midnight.

LINLEY. At the inn?

CHARLES. Yes. By candlelight!

LINLEY. For heaven's sake!

SHERIDAN. I presume from the quantity of bandage he is wearing that you consulted a surgeon?

CHARLES. He has a wound in his arm and another in his chest. I thought at first the sword had pierced his heart, but I was mistaken.

ALICIA (*horrified*). Oh!

RICHARD (*weakly*). It would have done so, only that the blade was turned aside by the frame of Elizabeth's picture——

ALICIA. Do you wear it on your heart?

RICHARD. Always!

SHERIDAN. And where, may I ask, have you been since then?

CHARLES. We engaged a room at the inn and went to sleep.

SHERIDAN. You what——!

CHARLES (*coming to above the settee*). You see, Richard had not been to bed since he left France. The surgeon said that was why he fainted——

SHERIDAN. Indeed! Since, then, he is adequately refreshed, and has no further plans for the evening, perhaps *I* may be allowed to claim a few moments of his attention—Shelah!

SHELAH (*down* R.). Yes, sir.

SHERIDAN. You are the oldest member of this household. I have trusted you and you betrayed my trust. What explanation have *you* to offer for your conduct?

SHELAH (*sulkily*). Master Richard asked me to go with him.

SHERIDAN. *I* asked you to take control of my family, to protect and care for my defenceless daughter.

(*His children look at each other and sigh.*)

It seems to me that what Mr. Richard asks means more to you than what I—your master—have enjoined.

SHELAH. Didn't he persuade me against my better judgment?

SHERIDAN. That is not a serious explanation——

SHELAH. Sure, don't you know by this that the same young man could talk a hole through an iron pot!

SHERIDAN. You old scarecrow! Is that all you have to say for yourself?

SHELAH. Ah, musha, I always did take rare delight in the tender passions!

SHERIDAN (*almost speechless*). With a face like *that*?

SHELAH (*going*). Me face is me own, and when I look at yours this minute, I thank God for the one I've got!

(*She goes out* R. *with a flourish.*)

SHERIDAN (*collecting his dignity*). Ahem! That woman has a tongue like a serpent. I can't think why I put up with her.

LINLEY (*rising*). May I now be allowed to retire?

SHERIDAN. Just a moment, Mr. Linley. There is another matter. (*He waves his letters in the air.*) On my return I found these awaiting me. Do you know what they are? Bills! Everyone of them—bills!

LINLEY. But surely, Mr. Sheridan——

SHERIDAN. Wait, sir, wait.

(LINLEY *sits again.*)

RICHARD. You left us so little money, Father, I was

obliged to order certain necessaries for the journey to France.

SHERIDAN. Listen to the necessaries I am asked to pay for, Mr. Linley! (*Reading*.) "To a pair of neat foils, one guinea——" (*He returns each letter to the mantelpiece.*)

CHARLES. Those were for the duel.

SHERIDAN. "One neat hair locket; one pound, eleven and sixpence. One fancy ring; two pounds, twelve shillings and sixpence. One pair of neat garnet buttons; one pound fifteen. And "—pray mark this, Mr. Linley—" To fitting a picture in a case; three shillings and sixpence."

RICHARD. That picture frame saved my life!

LINLEY (*dryly*). Then it was undoubtedly cheap at the price.

SHERIDAN (*shuffling the bills angrily*). "To a sedan chair to the Crescent, and waiting three hours; four shillings."

ALICIA (*softly*). She was such a long time getting ready.

SHERIDAN. "To a private post-chaise from Bath to London; ten guineas "—*I* have to travel on the public coach. "To a book borrowed from the Bath Circulating Library, and not returned; ten shillings——" I presume that was to provide a little reading matter on the journey——

ALICIA. It was a book I lent to Elizabeth——

LINLEY. If it is in my house, it shall be sent back to you this very day. (*He rises.*)

SHERIDAN. A moment, Mr. Linley!

LINLEY (*replacing the chair* R.). I decline to remain another instant, sir. This enumeration of your financial liabilities is no concern of mine, except that I observe that you do not add my account for your daughter's singing lessons to the list. I must beg you to excuse me.

SHERIDAN (*crossing to* R.C.). No concern of yours, sir! The post-chaise hired at your daughter's instigation! The foils used to fight for your daughter's honour. These bills are by right *yours*, sir, not mine.

LINLEY. This is preposterous. Your son, and only your son, is responsible for these debts. Yes, and responsible for the financial loss that *I* have incurred by my daughter's absence—at *his* instigation—from the concerts for which she was engaged.

SHERIDAN (*to* RICHARD). Do you hear that, sirrah?

RICHARD. Yes, Father.

SHERIDAN. And what have you to say for yourself?

RICHARD. Mr. Linley is perfectly right——

SHERIDAN. What!

RICHARD. His responsibility in Elizabeth's flight is not financial—it is moral.

LINLEY. What!

RICHARD. As for the bills, tradesmen are notoriously grasping, and paying only encourages them.

SHERIDAN. ⎱ The double-dyed villain!
LINLEY. ⎰ The insolent young scoundrel!

(RICHARD *closes his eyes in elegant reproof. The door bursts open and* ELIZABETH *enters, followed by* POLLY *and* SHELAH.)

LINLEY. Elizabeth!

(RICHARD *jumps to his feet.*)

ELIZABETH (*going swiftly to him*). Dick, Dick, you're safe!

(*She falls weeping on his breast. He encircles her with his free arm.*)

RICHARD (*tenderly*). Were you anxious, dear heart?

LINLEY (*thundering*). Elizabeth!

(*She takes no notice.* POLLY *runs to* ALICIA *for support.*) What are you doing here?

POLLY (*down* R., *wide-eyed*). They told us Dick was killed.

LINLEY. Who brought you to Bath?

POLLY. We came on the coach.

LINLEY. The public coach. My daughters—alone! Where is your self-respect, Elizabeth?

ELIZABETH (*turning to him proudly*). Self-respect? It is my right to be here.

LINLEY. }
SHERIDAN. } Right?

(ELIZABETH *takes a paper from the bosom of her gown.*)

ELIZABETH (*superbly*). He is my husband!

CURTAIN.

SCENE 2

SCENE.—*The same room three days later.*

As the CURTAIN *rises*, RICHARD *is sitting* L. *on the settee with a large book open on his knees. His arm is still bandaged.* MRS. LINLEY *is seated in the chair below the hearth, netting a purse.* ELIZABETH *is sitting beside* RICHARD, *holding his hand.* POLLY, *on the footstool at his feet, is gazing up lovingly into his face.* ALICIA *is standing behind the settee, stroking his head.* SHELAH *has collected cups and saucers on to a tray. One cup she holds in her hand, reading a fortune out of it, to* ELIZABETH, *who listens with rapt attention.*

ELIZABETH. Yes, go on, Shelah!

SHELAH. And there's a grand surprise and a settlement right up to you.

ELIZABETH. What does that mean?

SHELAH. How the divil should I know? I'm only telling you what the leaves say here, and it's money, money, money.

MRS. LINLEY. And so it should be with tea that has cost fourteen and sixpence a pound.

RICHARD. Well, our fortune's a trifle vague, Betsy, but apparently it is eminently satisfactory.

SHELAH (*annoyed*). Ah, you can make fun of my fortune if you choose, Master Richard, but I was born with the gift of second sight. (*She lifts up the tray and makes for the door.*) And I know what's going to happen to the whole family of you. Can't you open the door, Miss Lissy, when you see my hands full?

(ALICIA *crosses to open the door* R.)

RICHARD. Bring up the newspapers as soon as they arrive, Shelah. I have asked for them to be sent here immediately the mail comes in.

SHELAH (R.). You seem very interested in the newspapers all of a sudden.

POLLY (*anxiously*). You're not expecting another challenge, Dick?

RICHARD. No, I merely wish to see whether I am alive or dead to-day. The press accounts are so very contradictory.

SHELAH (*ironically*). Isn't it a happy man you ought to be, Master Richard? As happy as a peacock with two tails to spread instead of one.

(*She goes out* R., *kicking the door after her.* ALICIA *returns to her place.*)

MRS. LINLEY (*dryly*). Are you completely happy, Richard?

RICHARD (*drowsily*). Supremely. Go on, Lissy. That is most soothing.

MRS. LINLEY. You should have Mr. Reynolds to paint your portrait in that position, Richard. It might be called "The Reward of Valour."

RICHARD. You are vastly unkind, Mrs. Linley.

MRS. LINLEY. Not at all, Richard. I have the greatest admiration for your talents. That is why I am here.

POLLY (*loyally*). Bath talks of nothing but you.

RICHARD. Not scandal, I hope?

ALICIA. Scandal?

POLLY. You're the hero of the town.

ELIZABETH (*fondly*). What scandal could they speak of *you*?

RICHARD. None, but the absence of material never daunts the people of this fair city. If there is nothing to hand they invent some. Bath is a regular school for scandal—zounds! (*He sits up excitedly.*) There's a title for a comedy! "The School for Scandal." I'll write it some day, "The School for Scandal."

POLLY (*eagerly*). What will it be about?

RICHARD. Us! Lovers, and duels, and angry fathers!

ELIZABETH (*doubtfully*). I think I would prefer you to be a lawyer, Dick. There is more future in it.

MRS. LINLEY. You leave Richard to himself, Elizabeth. That boy has genius in him. Who else could have sent Captain Matthews packing so successfully? The villain! Why, I think he would be stoned if he dared so much as to show his face in the streets of Bath. And look at those poems he wrote you! I'm like Shelah, I believe Richard was born to make a stir in the world.

ELIZABETH. You have been wonderfully kind to us, Mama. I only wish that Papa, too, approved of Dick.

MRS. LINLEY (*calmly*). He will, in time. I'll see to that.

RICHARD. Did you like the poem I sent you yesterday, my love?

ELIZABETH (*with a sigh*). Very, very much. (*She takes a paper from her bosom and looks at it.*) I know it by heart already.

RICHARD. Sing it to me. It goes to the tune of "Gramachree Molly." You know—— (*He mumbles out a few tuneless notes.*) Wow, wow, wow wow wow, wow——

ELIZABETH (*laughing*). What a great donkey you are when you try to sing! (*Rising.*) You know the air he means, Polly?

POLLY. Yes.

ELIZABETH. Come and play it for me.

(POLLY *goes to the harpsichord.*)

POLLY. It is thick with dust.

ALICIA. Plain to see that none of the Sheridans use it.

(POLLY *begins to play.*)

ELIZABETH (*singing*).
   Had I a heart for falsehood framed,
   I ne'er could injure you;
   For though your tongue no promise claimed
   Your charms would make me true.
   To you no soul shall bear deceit,
   No stranger offer wrong;
   But friends in all the aged you'll meet,
   And lovers in the young.

   But when they learn that you have blest
   Another with your heart,
   They'll bid aspiring passion rest,
   And act a brother's part.
   Then, lady, dread not here deceit,
   Nor fear to suffer wrong;
   For friends in all the aged you'll meet,
   And brothers in the young.

(*While she sings* SHELAH *opens the door to admit* LINLEY. *He makes a sign to her not to speak, and stands listening gravely. When the song is over, there is silence for a moment.* SHELAH *goes out quietly.*)

LINLEY (*quietly*). You are in good voice to-day, my dear.

ELIZABETH (*turning*). Papa!

(POLLY *rises*.)

LINLEY (*advancing to* L. *of the spinet*). That is a most harmonious air. I have always admired it. And the verses are both sincere and touching. Who wrote them?

MRS. LINLEY (*dryly*). Richard.

LINLEY (*crossing* C.). Oh—I see. I am somewhat surprised to find you all here——

MRS. LINLEY. Are you, Thomas?

LINLEY. Well—er—I——

ELIZABETH (*moving down* R.C. *holding out the paper*). Here are the verses, Papa. Would you like to read them?

G

LINLEY (*curtly*). No. I came to see Mr. Sheridan. Is he not at home?

RICHARD. He and Charles have gone to Clifton Hotwells on business.

(ALICIA *is above the settee.*)

ELIZABETH (*still holding the paper towards him*). The words accord excellently with the music. (*She hurriedly takes more papers from her frock.*) Here are others he wrote.

LINLEY (*looking at the papers for a second, then taking them abruptly.*) Indeed? (*He walks with them to the window.*)

RICHARD (*to* ELIZABETH). I'll put all my songs in an opera some day, and your father shall write the music.

ELIZABETH (*crossing below to the fire*). Castles in Spain!

RICHARD. And I'll set it in Spain to remind you of your lack of faith!

(MRS. LINLEY *lays her hand gently on* ELIZABETH'S *arm to draw her attention to* LINLEY *in the window. He is holding a paper in one hand, and striking imaginary notes with the other. Then he falls into a deep reverie.* RICHARD, POLLY *and* ALICIA, *who are talking, do not notice this little by-play.*)

POLLY (*moving and sitting at* R. *end of settee*). May I come and live with you when you are a famous author, Dick?

ALICIA. We'll all go and live with him.

RICHARD (*putting his arm round* ALICIA). What would Father and brother Charles say?

ALICIA (*laughing*). We shan't ask them.

POLLY. I should love to go on the stage. Will you give me a part to play?

RICHARD. I shall certainly endeavour to invent something sufficiently elegant and refined——

POLLY. I wish I were your wife instead of Elizabeth.

ALICIA. Polly!

RICHARD. I would marry you both if I could.

LINLEY (*folding the papers and moving* R.C.). Ahem! Yes, as you say, Elizabeth, there is an element of merit in the verses. With some—er—alterations, they might possibly be set to music. I will study them more carefully at my leisure, Richard.

RICHARD. You can see all I have written.

LINLEY. These will do for the present, thank you. One or two are quite—passable. I would like to try setting a little air—— (*He walks towards the door.*)

MRS. LINLEY (*quickly, rising and crossing* R.C.). What did you come to see Mr. Sheridan about?

LINLEY (R., *halting*). The matter, my dear Mary, was strictly private.

MRS. LINLEY (R.C.). Have you seen the lawyer?

LINLEY (*unwillingly*). Yes.

(ELIZABETH *crosses down* L.)

MRS. LINLEY. What did he say?

LINLEY. Really, Mary——

MRS. LINLEY. I am anxious to know.

(ALICIA *goes up* C.)

LINLEY (*looking uncomfortably at the young people, who are listening eagerly*). He thinks that in this country the marriage would probably *not* be considered legal.

MRS. LINLEY. But it might be——?

LINLEY (*very reluctantly*). It might.

RICHARD (*jumping to his feet*). Our marriage?

(POLLY *rises.*)

MRS. LINLEY. Yes.

RICHARD. We are perfectly agreeable to being married over again if it would make you happier, aren't we, Elizabeth?

(POLLY *goes to the fire.*)

ELIZABETH (*slightly bewildered*). Yes, Richard.

LINLEY (*dryly*). That is exceedingly kind of you both.

RICHARD (*crossing* C.). Not at all, we shall like it.

LINLEY. Not so fast, young man. If, at some future date, I should agree to another marriage—if I agree, I say——

MRS. LINLEY. Of course you'll agree. Richard is a match in a thousand.

LINLEY. Our opinions differ somewhat on that point.

MRS. LINLEY. Besides, you can't have your daughter half married and half a maid.

LINLEY. That is my one reason for even considering the marriage. If I do agree, Elizabeth must first promise to fulfil all the public engagements I have made on her behalf.

ELIZABETH (*moving* L.C.). I can't, I can't. Richard, don't let them make me sing in public again!

RICHARD. You shall never be obliged to do so, my love. Trust me in this.

LINLEY. The contracts were already signed before this—this form of marriage.

RICHARD. Elizabeth's marriage breaks every contract as completely as her death would have done. (*He taps his large book.*) I have studied sufficient law to know that.

LINLEY. But what about *my* loss, sir?

RICHARD. Your loss! Why, you have twenty more Elizabeths at home.

LINLEY. I have four more daughters, sir, including the twins, who are as yet unable to speak.

RICHARD. Well, you're both young yet. You've plenty of time.

LINLEY. Sir!

MRS. LINLEY (*laughing*). La! This is better than any play I ever saw in a theatre. (*She crosses* L.)

(SHELAH *bursts in* R.)

SHELAH. The master! He's coming upstairs.
RICHARD. What!
ELIZABETH. Oh!

(SHELAH *flattens herself against the door hoping to escape notice.*)

RICHARD. I'm sorry, Mrs. Linley.
MRS. LINLEY (*tartly*). And so you should be!
(POLLY *runs to her mother, who has risen in some haste.* ALICIA *tries to cross to the study door, but does not reach it in time.* ELIZABETH *shrinks closer to* RICHARD'S *side. He stands with his head held high as if prepared to withstand a dozen angry fathers. Only* LINLEY *is unperturbed. They are all standing staring at the door when* SHERIDAN *and* CHARLES *come in.* SHERIDAN *takes in the tableau with amazement.* SHELAH *slides out.*)

SHERIDAN (*thundering*). What is the meaning of this?
CHARLES (*amused*). It's quite a family gathering!

(*There is a pause.*)

SHERIDAN. Will no one explain the meaning of this—this visitation? Are you all dumb?
RICHARD. We did not expect you home for hours, Father.
SHERIDAN (*crushingly*). That is self-evident.
LINLEY (R.C.). I came to discuss my visit to the lawyer. You will remember that you, yourself, desired me to call immediately I had seen him. I was not aware that you intended to go to Hotwells.
SHERIDAN (R.). And may I ask if I also invited your wife and daughter? I seem to have no recollection of it!
LINLEY. They were here when I came. I am no more responsible for their presence than you are.
SHERIDAN (*grandly*). Far be it from me to wish to eject any female from my house, but I must ask Mrs. Linley to explain her presence here; after which she will, perhaps, oblige me by withdrawing.
MRS. LINLEY (*down* L. *with* POLLY). I came to act as duenna to my daughter, as any self-respecting mother would do.
SHERIDAN (*to* ELIZABETH). And you, Madam?
ELIZABETH (L.C.). I came to see Richard.
SHERIDAN. If my daughter ever chose to behave in so unmaidenly a fashion, I would lock her up.

(*The young* SHERIDANS *look at each other appreciatively.*)

ELIZABETH. But I am not a maiden, Mr. Sheridan. I am a wife!

SHERIDAN. Psha!

RICHARD. It's true, Father, the lawyer says so.

SHERIDAN. What!

CHARLES (C.). Bravo, Richard! Every man in England will envy you. (*He turns to* ELIZABETH.) My sister will forgive me saying that *I* do most heartily.

ELIZABETH. Thank you. (*She extends her hand.* CHARLES *kisses it gallantly.*)

SHERIDAN. The lawyer is a fool.

LINLEY. Richard misunderstands. The lawyer did not say the marriage was legal——

SHERIDAN (*impatiently*). Any other suggestion is absurd.

LINLEY. He said the legality is open to dispute.

SHERIDAN. Thank you. My mind is at rest. I wish you and your family a very good day. I trust we shall never meet again. (*He flings open the door.*)

ALICIA. Father——

SHERIDAN (*shouting*). Silence.

(ALICIA *subsides.*)

LINLEY. Come, Mrs. Linley——

MRS. LINLEY (*moving to* L.C.). Just a moment, Mr. Sheridan. You appear to forget that my daughter's reputation is at stake.

SHERIDAN (*down* R.). Your daughter should have thought of that before she persuaded my son to elope with her——

RICHARD (L.C.). Father!

SHERIDAN (*crossing* C.—*furiously*). If you persist in this ridiculous courtship I will disown you. No son of mine shall ever marry a fiddler's daughter.

LINLEY (R.C., *angrily*). Then we are at last agreed, sir, for no daughter of mine shall ever marry a player's son. I bid you good day, sir. Come, Mrs. Linley.

ELIZABETH (*pleading*). Dick!

RICHARD (*seriously*). Nothing can ever part us now, Elizabeth; you need not be afraid. Mr. Linley, I love your daughter. I ask you formally for the honour of her hand. I have no means of livelihood except the talents I feel myself to possess.

(SHERIDAN *exclaims impatiently.*)

But I swear to you here and now, that I shall not rest until I have won such a place in the world that my wife will be acknowledged equal of the highest ladies in the land. I promise you, Mr. Linley, and (*turning to his father*) you too, sir, that one day the Prince of Wales himself will be honoured to claim the friendship of the fiddler's daughter and the player's son!

CHARLES (*above the settee, clapping his hands*). An excellent curtain speech, Richard. Make a note of it, before you forget it. (*He moves to below the settee.*)

MRS. LINLEY (*admiringly*). It is an actor you should be, Richard, not a playwright.

(POLLY *sits below the fire.*)

LINLEY (*dryly*). Not an actor, Mrs. Linley, an orator! He should go into Parliament.

SHERIDAN (*crossing* L. *below the settee*). I am deeply hurt by your levity, Charles. I expect more consideration from you than from your brother.

CHARLES. I am sorry, sir. (*He moves up* L. *of settee to the window, to beside* ALICIA.)

RICHARD (R.C.). Will you give us your consent, Mr. Linley?

LINLEY (R.). If I ask you to wait a little longer, a year or two——

RICHARD. That is a lifetime.

LINLEY. Six months, then. If, at the end of that time, Elizabeth still wishes to marry you, I will agree. It rests with her. In the meantime, she must fulfil the engagements I have made for her. These are my conditions.

RICHARD (*crossing* L.C.). Can you bear them, Elizabeth?

ELIZABETH (L.). I can bear anything so long as it leads to you.

RICHARD. After we are married, I swear you shall never sing for payment again.

SHERIDAN (C.). You appear to have settled everything, Mr. Linley. May I ask if you have also arranged how these two young fools are going to live?—that is if Richard can stay constant for six months, which I greatly doubt.

LINLEY. Richard will follow his profession, I presume. He should make an excellent lawyer.

RICHARD. I do not intend to practise law, I am going to be a writer—a dramatist!

SHERIDAN (*very grandly*). Then I wash my hands of you, Richard. When you are begging in the streets, remember that I did my best for you. I have educated you as handsomely as my means would allow. I have chosen for you the most honourable and lucrative profession that is open to the sons of a man who is without riches or influence. I have laboured with every ounce of my strength to save you from the fate that has been mine—the thankless task of winning applause in the theatre.

RICHARD. You have won as much applause as any actor living, Father—Garrick only excepted.

SHERIDAN (*sadly*). Garrick only excepted. Ah, there's the rub—my fame must be second to Garrick's.

RICHARD. Why shouldn't I also win a place for myself in the theatre?

SHERIDAN. I have found the theatre to be the house of poverty, indignity and heartbreak. I am a scholar, but men do not recognize my scholarship. I am a gentleman, but who is there in the orchestra or the gallery who would admit it? When you enter the playhouse you lose your status for ever. To yourself you may be the last of a line of kings, but to the audience you are nothing but a rogue and a vagabond. Never shall child of mine enter that doomed profession. If you persist you shall be son of mine no longer. (*He goes up* L.)

RICHARD (*moving up* C.). I cannot help myself——
LINLEY. You seem to be unduly positive of your talent, young man.
RICHARD (*passionately*). I know it is in me, and by God it shall come out!
SHERIDAN. Then I disown you. Henceforth I have only one son; you Alicia have only one brother——
ALICIA (*crossing down* R.). But, Father——
SHERIDAN (*holding up his hand*). I have said it. The foolhardy youth who calls himself Richard Sheridan is no relation of mine or of yours.
RICHARD. You will regret this sternness when I am famous, Father.
SHERIDAN. When you are famous—you impudent scoundrel! Come, Charles, we will withdraw to the other room until our—guests have departed. (*Crossing to* RICHARD.) I trust that you, sir, will soon follow their example, and relieve my house of your presence. Until the date of your examinations I will see that you do not starve; after that my obligation to you will be at an end, and thenceforth you may look to yourself, for I shall never help you. Follow me, Alicia.

(*He strides towards his study door* L.)

RICHARD (*running before him*). Father!
SHERIDAN (*furiously*). Out of my way! I have finished with you! (*He goes out majestically.*)
CHARLES. You had better arrange to be a failure, Dick. He'll never forgive you if you do succeed.
SHERIDAN (*outside*). Charles! Alicia!
CHARLES. Yes, Father.

(*He hurries out* L.)

ALICIA (*throwing her arms around* RICHARD). Henceforth I have only one brother—but Father doesn't know which it is!

(*She tears herself away and hurries out* L.)

ELIZABETH (*crossing up* L. *of settee to* L. *of him.*) Don't look so sad, Richard. You still have *me*.

POLLY (*crossing up* C. *to* R. *of him*). And me.

RICHARD. I'm very fond of Lissy.

ELIZABETH. She'll soon find a way to circumvent your father.

RICHARD (*brightening*). Yes, of course she will.

LINLEY (*who has gone to the door*). After what Mr. Sheridan has said, I have no wish to remain a moment longer, so if Richard will be so kind as to ask his servant to show us out, we will leave at once. (*He opens the door down* R.)

RICHARD (*disappointed*). Yes, sir.

(RICHARD *goes to the door* R. *and leans over the banisters.*)

RICHARD (*calling*). Shelah! Be ready to show Mr. Linley out.

ELIZABETH (*crossing* R.). You will let him call to see me, Papa?

MRS. LINLEY. Naturally.

RICHARD (*coming back*). Sir, I wanted to ask you——

LINLEY. If you have anything further to say, you may wait upon me at nine o'clock to-morrow morning. I wish to hear no more now. Good day.

(*He goes out* R. RICHARD *and* ELIZABETH *look at each other.*)

MRS. LINLEY (*with grim humour*). I will delay your father at the door two minutes, Elizabeth, not a moment longer.

(*She goes out* R. POLLY *pauses, gazing at them innocently.*)

POLLY (C.). She means that you may kiss him, if you like, Elizabeth.

ELIZABETH (*in a low voice*). I know.

POLLY. Aren't you going to?

ELIZABETH. Please go away.

POLLY (*going* R.). But you needn't mind me.

ELIZABETH. You don't understand——

POLLY (*to* RICHARD). What don't I understand?

RICHARD (*down* R.). Run away, Polly. You'll know all about it when you grow up.

POLLY (*suddenly bursting into tears*). I don't want to grow up now. Nothing will ever be the same again.

(*She runs out weeping.*)

RICHARD (*looking after her*). Poor little Polly! I must find her someone as like myself as possible.

ELIZABETH (*fondly*). You are very conceited, Richard.

RICHARD (*drawing her towards him*). If I were truly conceited, I would think that there could never be anyone like me. (*Seriously.*) There can never be anyone like you.

ELIZABETH (*almost sadly*). I do love you, Dick. I wish I knew that you loved me so well.

RICHARD (R.). My heart's darling. How can you doubt me?

ELIZABETH (R.C., *looking up at him*). You're so clever, and I am only an ignorant girl. I wish now that my father had trained me to be a blue-stocking.

RICHARD. God forbid! I hate women link-boy-like.

(*They laugh a little and then fall silent. They cross* L. *to the settee.*)

ELIZABETH (*softly*). Now I shall sing only for you, Dick—and you'll never understand how much I mean to say.

(*They kiss.* SHELAH *comes in* R.)

SHELAH. Your father is bawling for you below stairs, Mrs. Sheridan.

ELIZABETH. Mrs. Sheridan! Oh, Richard, soon everyone will be calling me that.

SHELAH. So you've got round the old ones, after all?

ELIZABETH (*proudly*). We are going to be married—really, I mean—in six months.

SHELAH. Ah, the grand courage of the young! He'll fret you to death, Mrs. Sheridan, that he will. Playboy he ever was, and playboy he ever will be. That sort is like the fairies, they never properly grow up.

ELIZABETH (*crossing* C., *smiling at her*). You must

come and live with us, Shelah, and help me to manage him.

RICHARD (L.C.). Certainly! Though heaven alone knows where we shall find her wages. We are going to be very poor, my love.

ELIZABETH (*proudly*). I would rather have you with poverty than any other man with a throne.

RICHARD (*very moved*). Dear heart, dear love!

(*They kiss again.*)

(SHELAH *throws her hands up, and, hurrying out, looks anxiously over the banisters.*)

LINLEY (*below*). Elizabeth!

(RICHARD *and* ELIZABETH *do not hear. They remain clasped in each other's arms.*)

CURTAIN.

PROPERTY PLOT

ACT I

SCENE 1

Music on harpsichord.
Book on harpsichord.
Ink, pens, writing-paper, key, on bureau.
Duster under cushion on window-seat L.
Off Stage, R.
    Decanter of sherry for MRS. LINLEY.
    Three books for SHELAH.
Off Stage, L.
    Basket with concert tickets for POLLY.
    Tray with glasses for MRS. LINLEY.
    Small laudanum bottle for ALICIA.
Effects.
    Violin off L.
    Dog bark off L.
    Door knock off R.
    Door bang off R.

SCENE 2

Curtains closed.
Strike drinks and basket of concert tickets.
See that laudanum bottle is on table up R.C.
Two candles (lit) on harpsichord, also music script paper.
Move table C. to down R., and add on it: one candle (lit), taper, music and music paper, ink, pen.
Put stool from bureau to table down R.
Put chair down L. to below harpsichord with heap of music on it.
Off Stage, R.
    Library book for ALICIA.
    Bundle of letters for MATTHEWS.
Effects.
    Door knock off R.
    Door bang off R.

ACT II

SCENE 1

Pewter ink-pot, sand drying-pot, RICHARD's hat, on table L.C.

Off Stage.
  Register with sheet of foolscap written on for CURÉ.
  Prayer-book for CURÉ.
  Wedding-ring for RICHARD.
  Special Bath newspaper for CHARLES.
  Prayer-book for MÈRE MARIE.
  Purse with coins for LINLEY.

Effects.
  Horse and wheel.
  Big bell.
  Bolt and chain.

SCENE 2

Two pens, ink, writing-paper, candlesticks (lit), on desk down L.
Belts, spurs, sword, pistols, rag and oil for cleaning, powder flask, on table C.

Off Stage.
  Tray with bottle of brandy and glass for LANDLORD.
  Lantern (lit) for LANDLORD.
  Sheet of plain paper for RICHARD.
  Swords for RICHARD.
  Documents and bundle of letters tied up for MATTHEWS.

Effects.
  Knocker and mallet.

ACT III

SCENE 1

Clock, candle (lit), seven special tradesmen's accounts, on mantelpiece.

Off Stage R.
  Sheets of foolscap, marriage certificate, for ELIZABETH.

SCENE 2

Add cushion to settee.
Bring table from up L.C. to down L.C. and add tea-tray and four empty, but used, cups, saucers and spoons.
Strike armchair C.
Large law book for RICHARD.
Tatting for MRS. LINLEY.
Three pieces of paper with poems written on them for ELIZABETH.

112 MISS LINLEY OF BATH.

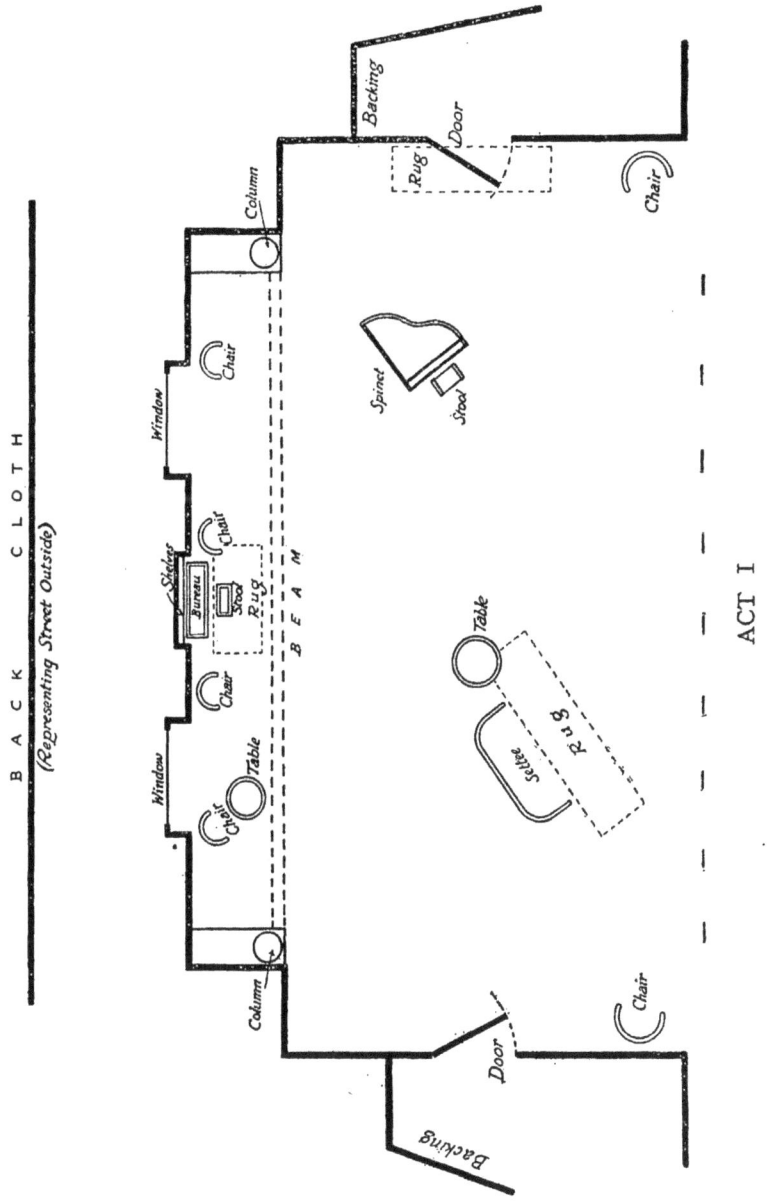

ACT I

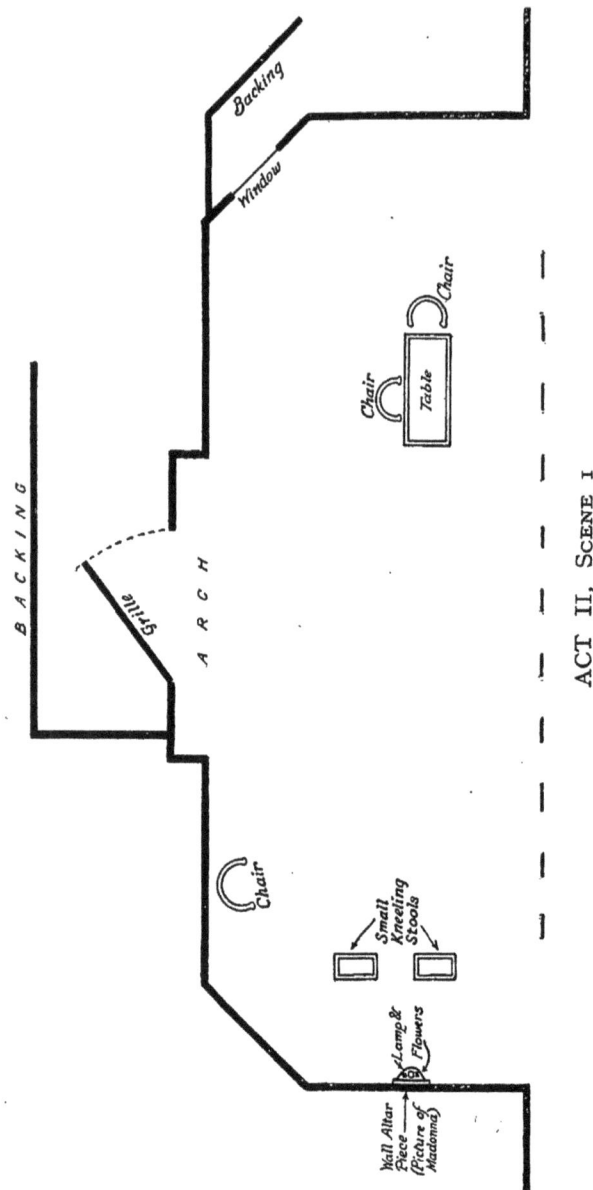

ACT II, SCENE I

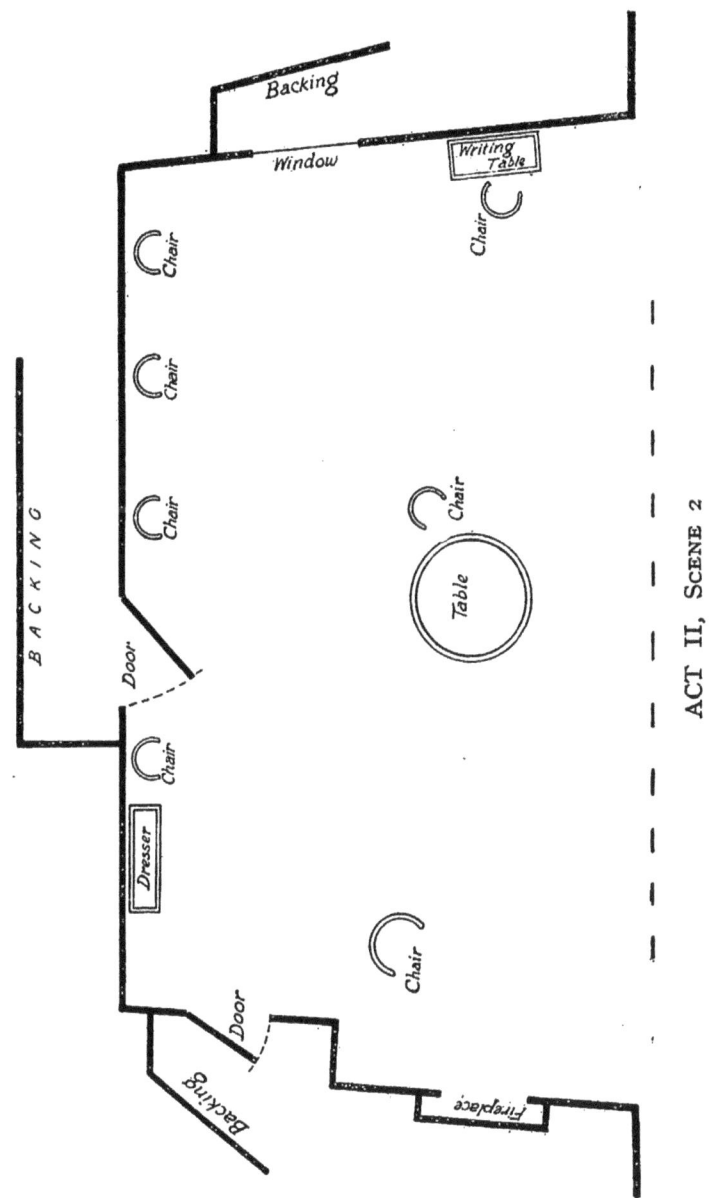

ACT II, SCENE 2

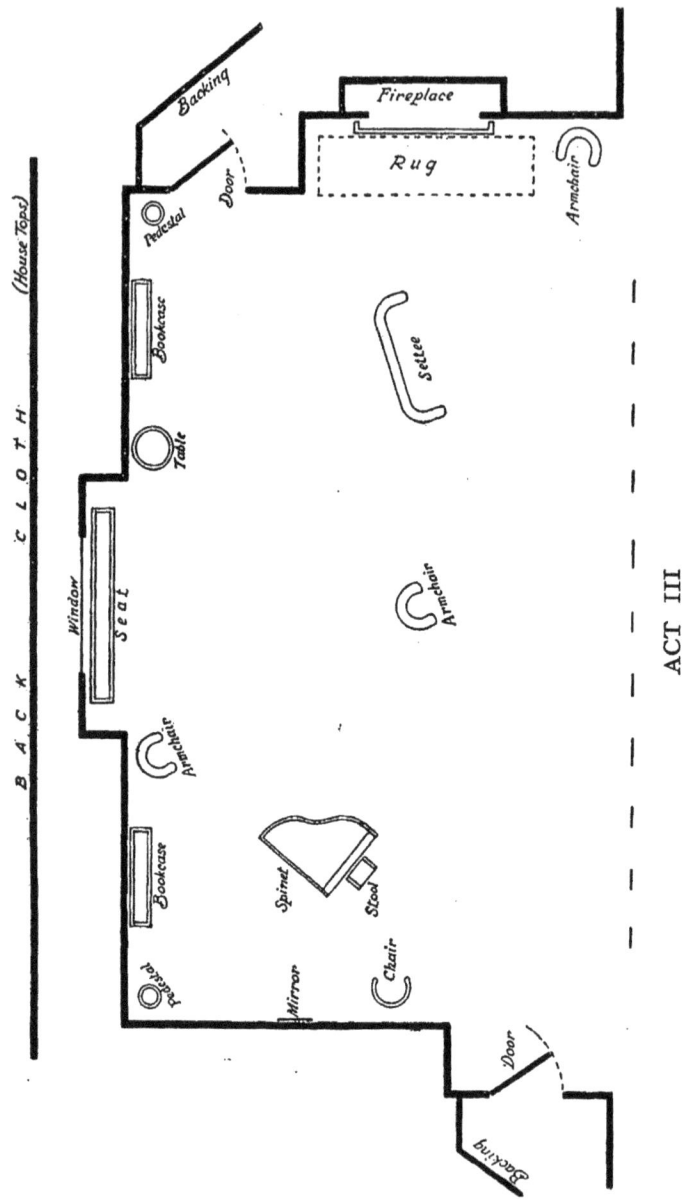

ACT III

www.ingramcontent.com/pod-product-compliance
Ingram Content Group UK Ltd.
Pitfield, Milton Keynes, MK11 3LW, UK
UKHW021843210426
5322IPUK00022B/441